WALKING
BRITAIN'S MOST BEAUTIFUL NATURE TRAILS

1
West of England

2
South East and East Midlands

3
Wales and West Midlands

4
North of England

5
Central and South Scotland

6
North of Scotland

Each walk is listed in the Contents under one of four different categories:
Countryside; Seaside; Forest and Woodland and River and Lakeside.
Each entry is prefixed by a regional number – a simple way to spot your ideal walk.

SYMBOLS USED ON TRAIL MAPS

Parking

P

Start

Viewpoint

Toilets

T

Picnic area

✗

A WORD OF THANKS

This edition published 1992 by the Promotional Reprint Company
Limited for Bookmart Limited, Desford Road, Enderby, Leicester, UK.

Printed and bound in Hong Kong.

The contents of this book are believed to be correct
at the time of printing. Nevertheless, the publisher
cannot accept any responsibility for errors or
omissions, or for changes in details given.

ISBN 1 85648 048 8

JUST A WORD

BY PHIL DRABBLE

I am a confirmed leaner-over-gates. A lifetime's experience has taught me that I see more of interest, in five minutes, standing still and quiet, than in hours of wandering aimlessly about.

Sudden movement or staccato noise startles everything, so that what is vibrant with life one moment will be a dull vacuum the next. I discovered, at an early age, that the most rewarding walks consist of a studied syncopation of progress and immobility.

It is no good, though, leaning over a gate that overlooks nothing of interest, and the purpose of this book is to direct readers' feet in the most rewarding directions, where the widest possible range of interests is satisfied.

The breathtaking scenery of remote and rugged mountains is even more memorable to the background music of lilting curlews or the sexy challenge of red stags at rutting time. The primitive appeal of water can suit any mood, depending on whether it is the solitude of mountain tarns, graceful yachts, on man-made reservoirs or the irresistible power of breakers pounding rocky coasts.

Walking caters for the widest range of interests and moods. There are trails through dense coniferous forests and the ancient deciduous woodlands that were here before our earliest ancestors.

My own favourite countryside happens to be the variegated patchwork of pasture and arable fields, punctuated by the woods and copses which our forefathers planted, not for profit, but for sport; the odd clumps of cover from which they drove high pheasants across deep valleys or foxes to run the gauntlet before their hounds.

The stately homes in such rich countryside, are a link with a past which was spacious and leisurely and prosperous.

There is plenty in this book for quite different tastes. Not only has the object been to select trails which include the broadest canvas of habitat, but each trail has as varied a set of features as possible.

Some trails are administered by naturalists' organisations, others by National Park authorities, the Forestry Commission or even the commercial interests of Country Parks or houses open to the public. For good measure, there are also gazetteered entries of other trails within ten or twenty miles of each selected site.

One of the obvious dangers of our mechanical age is that it is all too easy to kill the very things we love by the sheer pressure of the numbers of people who wish to enjoy them. The erosion of tens of thousands of pairs of feet in the Peak National Park or on Snowdon or Dartmoor are obvious examples.

Shy creatures, like otters, have grown scarce partly because of the destruction of their habitat by drainage boards or as a result of eating prey suffering the effects of poisonous pesticides, but they have also grown scarce because so many people throng river banks, where they once lived, that the seclusion they needed to breed has vanished.

Yet our modern nostalgia for simple things and quiet places has generated the strength of public opinion that has forced politicians to limit the use of poisons on the land and to pass laws to protect our threatened species and ancient buildings and glorious landscape.

It is a delicate balance and, by describing such a wide range of interests in the trails in this book, the load can be spread more thinly instead of being concentrated in fewer, more hackneyed spots.

Even more important is the stress laid on the conservation aspects of the trails described and the civilised behaviour that will result in their being enhanced instead of destroyed.

I hope that readers will derive great benefit from it – and that the trails described will profit as a result.

Phil Drabble

CONTENTS
AND REGIONAL MAP

FOREST AND WOODLAND WALKS

COUNTRYSIDE WALKS

SEASIDE WALKS

RIVER AND LAKESIDE WALKS

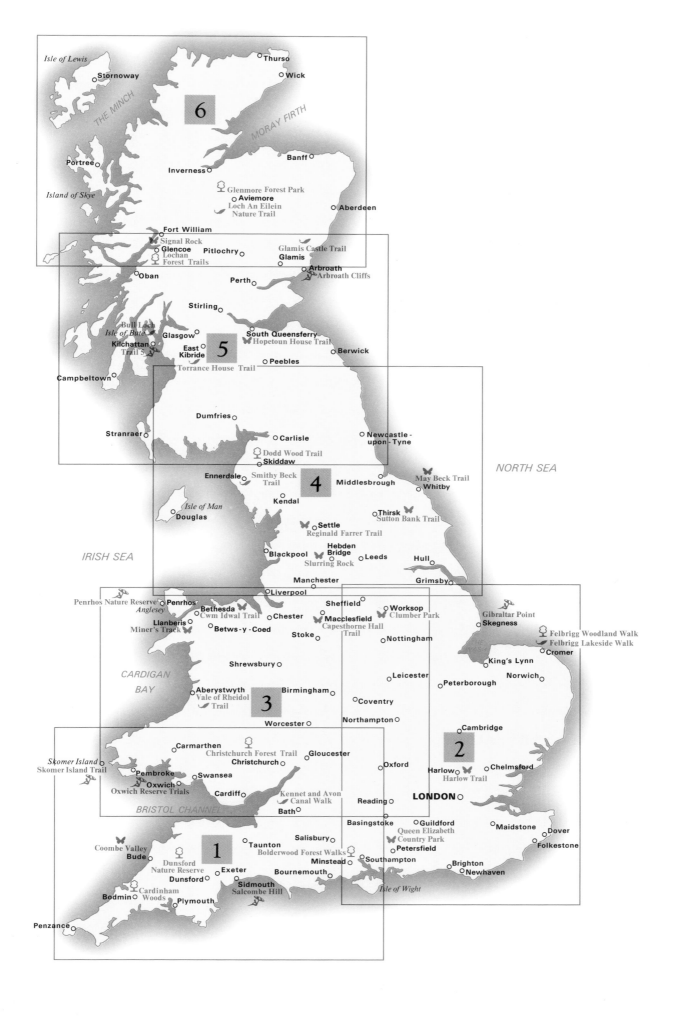

Location Map

Scale : 45 miles to 1 inch

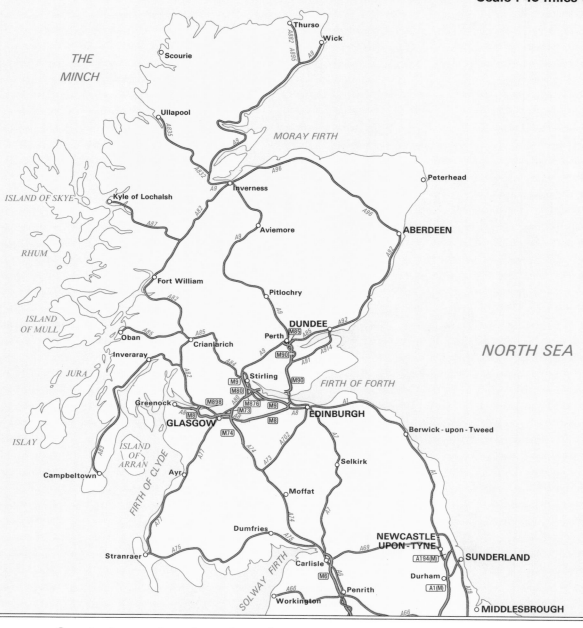

THE MINCH

MORAY FIRTH

ISLAND OF SKYE

RHUM

ISLAND OF MULL

JURA

ISLAY

ISLAND OF ARRAN

FIRTH OF CLYDE

SOLWAY FIRTH

FIRTH OF FORTH

NORTH SEA

Thurso
Wick
Scourie
Ullapool
Inverness
Peterhead
Kyle of Lochalsh
Aviemore
ABERDEEN
Fort William
Pitlochry
Oban
Crianlarich
Perth
DUNDEE
Inveraray
Stirling
Greenock
GLASGOW
EDINBURGH
Berwick - upon - Tweed
Campbeltown
Ayr
Selkirk
Moffat
Dumfries
NEWCASTLE UPON - TYNE
SUNDERLAND
Stranraer
Carlisle
Durham
Penrith
Workington
MIDDLESBROUGH

Symbols used on location plans

M3 S	Motorway		Angling	†	Church
▰ ▰ ▰ ▰	Motorway under construction		River and lakeside walks	✳	Gardens, Parks
	Primary route		Countryside walks	✕	Windmill
	'A' road		Forest and woodland walks	🏛	Manor, Museum, House, Hall
	'B' road		Seaside walks		Priory, Abbey
	Unclassified	▲	Campsite	⚐	Golf
A40	Road number		Castle		

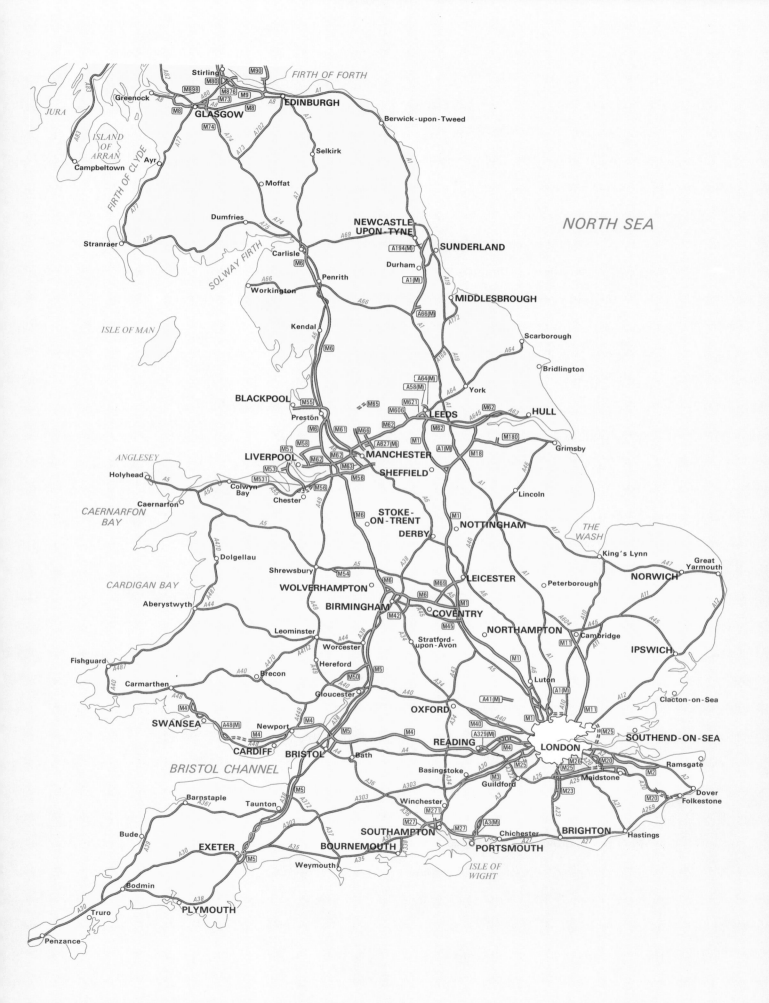

THE DO-IT-YOURSELF NATURE TRAIL

While the official nature trail is a delightful way of capturing the complete natural history spectrum in a unique habitat, flora and fauna do not stop at the trail car park. Every walk you take, be it only to the supermarket, can reveal a treasure trove of natural phenomena if you just open your eyes to it. The planned nature trail, now so much a part of the modern country park, forest leisure areas and nature reserves, is much more than a pleasant leisure amenity. It is a powerful educative force, teaching by example the interdependence that exists between all living things. In its unhurried progress from habitat to habitat, through stimulating surroundings it offers the relaxation of a contemplative stroll with the added interest of pointing out the denizens of the countryside – all neatly labelled for the benefit of the inquisitive.

Nature trails like this are so useful and interesting that it is very easy for the leisure-bent visitor to miss a very obvious point. That is, without the maps and markers, the wildlife brochures and the pathside notices describing the trail's more interesting features, these are all ordinary walks in the country. Think about it – a nature trail could be laid down anywhere. It could be in a town park, in the verges and gardens of a busy city, through the back garden of a tiny Victorian terrace or on the wild, windy tops of moorlands. Even in a window box, fifteen storeys above a city street are those same clues to the cycle of plant and animal life. The only difference is that there are no maps and signboards – the observer has to learn how to look, recognise and appreciate.

It is surprising how quickly you can assimilate the knowledge to make a start on your do-it-yourself nature trail. The names and form of a few plants found on an official trail may be your starting point but you can follow up your researches at the local library. Most libraries have abundant shelves of natural history books but what you should really search for are the slim volumes and pamphlets contributed by local natural history clubs and amateur and professional biologists. These will tell you the real curiosities to look for in your district.

Some places, of course, are much more interesting than others. While it may be possible to identify half a dozen plants and a few animals and insects when walking to work in a city street, there are literally thousands of species to be found along footpaths, woodland rides or green lanes. The less disturbed an environment remains, the more the variety of flora and fauna and the more natural patterns of interdependency develop. Your DIY nature trail should include some habitats where man has rarely trodden and where you, too, do not need to disturb the environment to make your observations.

This is not such a paradox as it may at first appear. Perhaps the most natural place of all which is never disturbed is the hedge bottom and this is somewhere that you need not enter to observe. Similar completely wild habitats are to be found at disused canal fringes (and the other side of the towpath), established coppices and shooting boxes, roadside and field ditch bottoms and in worked-out quarries.

Hedges are particularly good. They are usually very old and the fact that they are usually the only cover for quite a distance makes them ideal sanctuaries between tracts of open ground or roads for many species of wildlife. The hedge itself is a showcase of natural flora. The long, silver-grey stems of ash carry their distinctive black buds above spiky hawthorn and tangled masses of dogrose and bramble. Protected saplings spring from seeds and fruits dropped by birds and the whole bouquet may be bound by the sinuous strands of columbine, hop or honeysuckle. Smaller, less shrub-like plants grow in the darkness of the underhedge and in the grass-shrouded depths of the ditch which usually runs alongside.

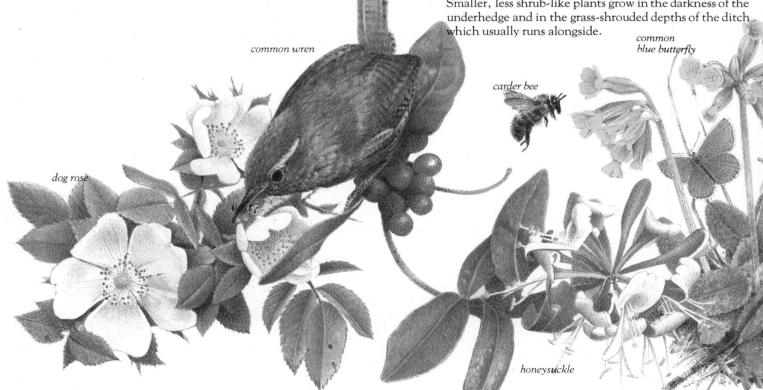

common wren

dog rose

carder bee

common blue butterfly

honeysuckle

Like any other environment or habitat, the seasons wreak their changes on the hedgerow. Spring brings pale primroses and violets among the moss tufts and songbirds nest in the blossoming thorn. By summer the ditch and verge are hidden by great trunks of cow parsley bearing their dusty umbels of flowers and sometimes surmounted by a towering stand of the look-alike hogweed. In autumn, the nut bushes and blackberry bear their fruit, which with the scarlet splash of briony and rowan berries, present a rich harvest for finches, tits, occasional squirrels and wintering mice.

As the green drops away at winter's approach, evidence of the hedgerow's larger inhabitants comes to light. Fresh burrows dug by a new generation of rabbits, the small excavations of mice and rats and the quick scurry of the hunting weasel may be seen.

River banks are equally fascinating places to the observer with a few minutes to spare. The fringe of mud between water and bank is a strange no-man's land where plants and animals which are neither completely aquatic nor entirely comfortable on land can be found.

After spring spawning, tiny frogs no bigger than half-penny pieces prey to fish and fowl alike make their appearance. Coots and moorhens quietly patrol their forests of yellow flag, reeds and water iris and busy mallards escort their yellow charges from cover to cover. You may spot the beautifully woven nest of a reed warbler, the predatory shadow of a pike patrolling the boundary between deep water and the fry-infested shallows or the superfast electric-blue flash of the kingfisher. Keep your ears as well as your eyes open to catch the distant booming call of the bittern, the rasping bellow of the toad and the rustle of the busy water rat.

On hot summer days the sweet, pervasive scent of watermint lies on the water like a mist and the great yellow bowls of water lilies float among the enormous green pads of their leaves.

Woodland walks are full of rustlings and quick movements just caught from the corner of the eye. The mature deciduous trees, usually oak or beech in natural woodlands, provide a broad green canopy alive with noise of invisible birds. Dead branches and rotten patches of wood open up the holes that are used by woodpeckers, nuthatches, starlings and tree-creepers – birds of the mid-forest habitat. High overhead are the untidy twig piles of a rook colony, while amid the thicket of birches and holly, spindly saplings and outgrown hazel coppice are tight nests of smaller birds. In the crotches of trees are the balls of leaves which form the grey squirrel's winter home and among taller thorny trees such as the crab-apple, magpies and jays make their untidy bases. Wood pigeons entrust their safety to small flat twig platforms.

The forest floor is usually a damp, shady place where the delicate wood anemone blooms, where Solomon's seal hangs its small, pearl-like flowers from curved stems winged with paired leaves and where thick bracken undergrowth masks the secret journeys of foxes, badgers and deer. Man's coniferous plantations – largely Sitka spruce – offer different attractions. The grey flash of a sparrow hawk may be caught as it hunts its tiny dashing quarry at head-height through the leafless pine trunks. On the needle-carpeted ground are the thin, delicate Christmas tree of a rare helleborine or the compact and highly detailed pyramid of an English orchid.

These are the ingredients of the DIY nature trail which can be followed in places near home or when away.

The seashore is a unique environment, chemically and climatically different to anywhere else in the country and full of highly specialised plants and creatures. Mountains and downlands have their own highly individualistic links between the colonies of flora and fauna on their slopes, as have open meadows, the vast lakelands of the Norfolk Broads and the microcosm of the village pond.

The keys to the enjoyment of your own nature trail are within the reach of everyone with the help of a handbook.

Solomon's seal

cowslip

stag beetle

dog wood violets

common frog

TREAD CAREFULLY ON NATURE'S TRAIL

The advent of the nature trail as a major countryside amenity is as much an expression of the need to guard against damage to the environment as a new means of adding interest to nature study. Here is how you can enjoy the sights and sounds of the countryside – and leave behind a beauty your children's children will visit with joy. 'To the woods, to the woods!', goes the old radio show joke – and it's never been truer than in the last decade. Man's increased mobility, the increase in leisure and the quest for a lungful of country air is placing terrific pressure on any accessible tract of countryside.

In response, the managers of Britain's outstandingly beautiful resources such as National Parks, forests, country estates and Nature Reserves have recognised the needs to awake leisure-bent man's interest in conservation, but equally enable the crowds to tread the paths where the sights are to be seen and least damage can be done.

That is where the undoubted success of the nature trail lies – it is both a vehicle of conservation and joy to wander over. So popular has it become, that a nature trail is an attraction in its own right at many of the commercial country parks which have become so much a part of the burgeoning countryside leisure market. It is doubtful whether anybody knows how many trails have been established within the last ten years. In the course of compiling this book, some 600 were discovered on lands as varied as the grounds of an aluminium smelter and a power station to the bankside of a railway and the towpath of a canal. Some are the carefully orchestrated results of conservationists' will to control public access to ecologically sensitive areas such as Nature Reserves. Others are the work of a dedicated local natural history group. All are shared by shepherded school groups, keen ornithologists and botanists, lone walkers and strolling families alike.

Unlike any other pastime, the right to enjoy the trail's environment and spot the many fascinating features detailed in the trail notes brings with it a responsibility to care for all the plants and animals that comprise this marvellous resort. On a nature trail the tenets of the Country Code bind even stronger if its features are to withstand the enormous pressures the visitations of man placed upon them. It is worth looking at the Code point by point to see its relevance to nature trails.

Guard against all risk of fire

Many of the trails in this book are designed in extensive Forestry Commission and private woodlands. The trees are not just there for birds to nest in – they are an extremely important renewable resource. A woodland which may take twenty-five to forty years to grow to an economic size can be wiped out in minutes by fire. Hundreds and thousands of acres of forest have been burned during the last few years because of the carelessness of visitors and the most vulnerable forests are those with the most visitors – the ones with the nature trails. However, as the big moor and brushland fires of 1976 showed, it is not just the trees that are at risk. Fire scars wherever it is set. As the Australian expression has it: 'One flaming match, no flaming trees!'.

If you *have* to smoke on a nature trail, sit down to do it, push the match head down into the earth to extinguish it completely and do the same with the cigarette end. Do not leave any glass around – it can focus the sun and ignite any dry material. Stop children playing with matches and fires and if necessary call a park warden. If you find a small fire, try to stamp it out. If it is out of control, call help immediately, and do not put yourself at risk – stay upwind of the fire.

Fasten all gates

Several trails in this book cross farmlands, so this advice has some relevance but it is not what a farmer would tell you. Ideally you should leave a gate as you find it – farmers often leave gates open for a purpose.

Keep dogs under proper control

Dogs are banned from many Nature Reserves as they can wreak havoc among nesting birds and, sensibly, on all the

trails in this book it would be best if all dogs were kept on a lead. In any case the dog should be on a lead if there is any farm stock about. Remember that farmers have the legal right to shoot any dog found worrying stock.

Keep to paths across farmland
Always keep to the nature trail path – to do otherwise would be like visiting an art gallery and walking all over the pictures. The plants and animals can only exist in their present interdependence undisturbed and your intrusion is only tolerated if you stick to the signed way.

Avoid damaging fences, walls and hedges
If you stick to the nature trail paths, you should use the stiles and gates provided for access but if you are striking out into the countryside at large this rule is very relevant. Farmers spend millions of pounds every year making good damage to their boundaries. Most expensive of all to repair and the easiest to damage, are drystone walls. If a farmer can find someone to do it, a drystone wall costs about £60 a yard.

Leave no litter
Litter is not just unsightly. Plastic bags are as dangerous to cattle as they are to young children and even the ring of a ring-pull can could find its way into the gullet of a grazing animal. Do not throw a single object on the ground – take it all home with you or find a litter bin.

Safeguard water supplies
People or animals will have to drink the water which you decide to paddle in or let the dog swim in. Water is a valuable resource not always available for recreation.

Protect wildlife, trees, plants
This is the key to your enjoyment of the countryside. Many species of plants and birds are at risk from the attentions of collectors and misguided leisure seekers. Under the provisions of the 1975 Conservation of Wild Creatures and Wild Plants Act it is illegal to dig up a plant or a tree without the owner's permission. You can pick some common flowers such as primrose and bluebell (*some you cannot*) but you should never dig them up.

Many birds enjoy the law's protection too, with fines of up to £500 for the taking of eggs. Perhaps the worst crime of all that man perpetrates on animals is that of subjecting them to stress. Sheer harassment – noise, chasing and dog-worrying – probably does more to upset the balance of nature than any other aspect of man's intrusion on the countryside.

Go carefully on country roads
Many of the nature trails are in remote parts of the country, accessible only by narrow lanes. It goes without saying that these are not roads on which you can speed along. They are the kind of roads that cyclists, walkers, horse-riders and slow farm vehicles use as well as being roads that are regularly crossed by both farm and wild animals. Keep your speed right down and keep well over to the left of the road. When parking, make sure there is enough room for other vehicles to get by and do not block up farm or field gates. Parking cars on verges can damage drainage systems and help to erode earth banks – try to find a hard standing for the car.

Respect the life of the countryside
The people who lay out nature trails recognise that town-dwellers have a right to enjoy the countryside – but, equally, in bestowing it, the country-dweller demands that he be allowed to live and work in peace. As the Countryside Commission says, 'The public is on trust in the Countryside and it is up to all of us to ensure that this trust is not misplaced.'

Your responsibility goes a little further than the Country Code. Like any other activity there are some sensible guidelines to follow in walking itself. While there are some trails in the book which never stray far from firm, level ground and do not take more than an hour or so to walk and appreciate, there are others that are long and strenuous, entering country that can be hostile.

Always wear good, stout shoes which are waterproof. On the longer walks you will probably find it better to wear woollen socks as these are much more absorbent and less abrasive than nylon and other modern fibres. You will be more comfortable and less prone to blisters if you follow this advice. On the higher trails in the mountains,

proper walking boots are advisable. These give grip over the rock paths and ankle support which not only makes the going less tiring, it could save you from injury.

Few of the trails in this book are in country that experiences very severe conditions, but for those that are – the Snowdonia and Cairngorms trails are examples – good lightweight waterproofs should be carried, an extra sweater for warmth is a good idea and the wise carry an emergency source of energy such as a chocolate bar or dried fruit.

These are the few guidelines that will enable you to appreciate the countryside so much more. Britain's Country Code may seem very unwieldy by the side of that of America which goes:

Take nothing but pictures

Leave nothing but footprints

Kill nothing but time

Both approaches are necessary to ensure that our right to enjoy the countryside is preserved and that there is some countryside to enjoy at all.

THE COUNTRY CODE

Guard against all risk of fire

Fasten all gates

Keep dogs under proper control

Keep to paths across farmland

Avoid damaging fences, hedges and walls

Leave no litter

Safeguard water supplies

Protect wildlife, plants and trees

Go carefully on country roads

Respect the life of the countryside

Ordnance Survey map references
As many of the trails featured in this selection have information or starting points that are off the beaten track, the full Ordnance Survey map reference for the access point is given in the trail data panel.

A full Ordnance Survey reference consists of a two-letter code (example: SU) placing the reference within a particular 100 kilometre square of Britain and a group of six figures pinpointing the place within a 1 kilometre square of the map. The reference is useful on the Ordnance Survey 1:50 000 scale maps (e.g. the Tourist series) and 1:25 000 scale maps (e.g. the Leisure series).

The first three figures of the reference are called the *easting* and the first two figures of the group indicate the western edge of the kilometre square in which the point lies (the grid lines are numbered top and bottom and on both sides of the map sheet). The third figure is the number of tenths of a kilometre the point lies to the east of that line.

The second set of three figures is called the *northing* and contains a two-figure pointer to the southern edge of the kilometre square and a final figure indicating the tenths of a kilometre to the north of the line that the point lies.
E.g. Halfway Station : 597574

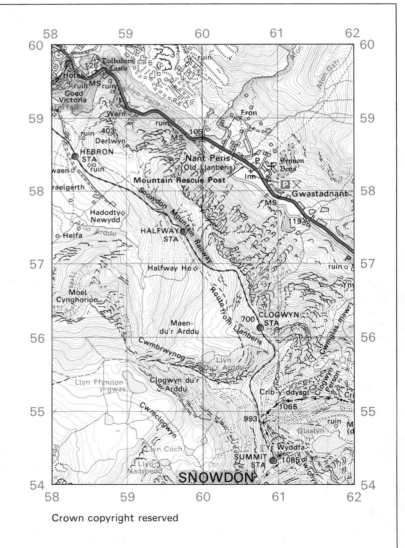

Crown copyright reserved

12

West of England 1

Coombe Valley Nature Trail

Cornwall Naturalists' Trust,
Malcolm S Henchley, Ferrers,
Stamford Hill, Bude, Cornwall

Off A39 unclassified road near to the hamlet of Coombe about 5 miles north of Bude

Map reference SS210118

1½-mile trail through wooded valley close to sea – easy to negotiate for young families

Facilities: Illustrated trail brochure from Trust and local tourism offices; small car parks nearby; cottages at trail start can be leased from the Landmark Trust

Inland from the bracing, salty winds of Cornwall's Atlantic Coast, the fields are grazed by dairy herds and cut by steep-sided lanes. It is country that is often discovered by car during the search for a quiet picnic spot or a country pub, so only the rampant dogrose and pink-freckled pyramids of foxglove are visible in the hedgerow. The rich treasure trove of Cornwall's natural history, cossetted by a warm and temperate climate, is unlocked only by those who park the car and take to the woods on foot.

Five miles to the north of the surf-bathing resort of Bude, is one such unbeaten track. The Coombe Valley Nature Trail, opened in 1970 by the North Tamar Region of the Cornwall Naturalists' Trust, is particularly suitable for families with young children. There are stiles, rather than main roads to negotiate.

Although only one-and-a-half miles long, the trail embraces an outstanding variety of plants and wildlife, and to see it all, and to absorb the attractive features of this sheltered valley, takes about two hours.

It is historically varied, too. For a number of centuries the land belonged to a notable Cornish family, the Grenvilles. The valley was their playground. As boys, Richard and Bevill would have ridden their horses through the woods and hawked and hunted with friends. Adult life was less idyllic. Sir Richard was killed defending his ship, the *Revenge*, against the Spanish in 1591; and fifty-two years later, Sir Bevill, a staunch Royalist, died at the Battle of Lansdown in 1643. During the 19th century, Robert S Hawker, vicar of Morwenstow and poet, took a wife twenty-two years his senior and honeymooned at Coombe Cottage. While there, he wrote *The Song of the Western Men*, which includes the much-quoted line 'And shall Trelawney die?'.

The Normans built a castle in the valley – probably without permission, as no official records list it – and it was later destroyed. Halfway along the trail is a pre-Roman earthwork.

On geological maps, this area is shaded sage green – the colour used for Culm Measures which belong to the relatively young (for rocks) Carboniferous period. At that time, most of the British Isles was below sea level, but after aeons of faulting and folding, the land was raised and a mixture of shales and sandstones became dry land. The soil is mainly clay with a top dressing of organic-rich humus which supports teeming plant-life. A stream flows through the valley and out to the grey, shale-strewn beach at Duckpool; the soil it collects along the way is deposited over the valley floor and kept there by lush grassland. Evidence of past structural activity can be seen at two places along the walk where anticlines expose layers of shale.

From the car park, the trail crosses a bridge over the stream and passes a mill and a cluster of cottages. Built in 1842, the three-storey mill was in use until fairly recently when the mighty water wheel turned two pairs of millstones, each four-feet thick. The miller and his

The coast near Bude

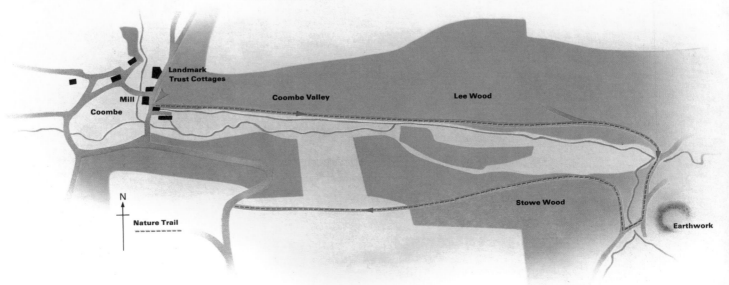

workers occupied the cottages – these days they can be hired through the Landmark Trust.

At first, the trees overhead are coppiced oaks, their true shapes contorted by the need for ships' timbers and fuel. The moist earth beneath encourages hart's tongue and shield fern, with its curious brown measle-like spores on the underside of each frond. Mossy banks are encroached upon by the ambitious thrust of brambles, while shiny ivy and fragrant honeysuckle grow upward, curling their supple shoots around tree trunks.

On the other side of a stile, the path enters Lee Wood – Stowe Wood is on the opposite side of the valley. These coniferous plantations work for their living and are part of the Hartland Forest – 2 700 acres planted by the Forestry Commission for timber production. Here the forest floor is carpeted with cones and pine needles, it is quieter than the oak wood, except for the odd rustle of a tiny shrew or a squirrel, or alarm from above as a magpie takes flight.

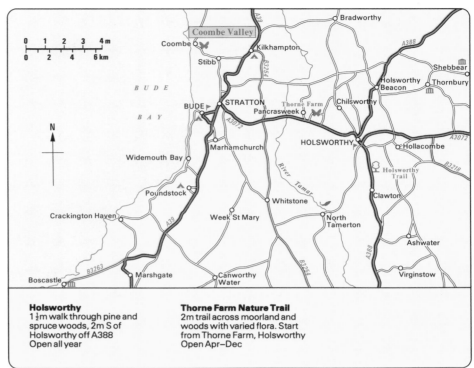

Holsworthy
1½m walk through pine and spruce woods, 2m S of Holsworthy off A388
Open all year

Thorne Farm Nature Trail
2m trail across moorland and woods with varied flora. Start from Thorne Farm, Holsworthy
Open Apr–Dec

Of all the many birds that inhabit Coombe Valley, the most dominant is the buzzard and the smallest of them all is the goldcrest.

Skirted by the golden-crowned spikes of gorse and through another oak coppice, the trail passes a spring, often dry in summer, and a hole high up in the bank, made by paper wasps. Heading south, the walker re-crosses the stream only two-and-a-half miles from its source. Damp spots foster the creamy clusters of meadowsweet and tall, pink Indian balsam, and the water itself has a dependent colony of creatures. The marsh fritillary butterfly might flirt with the sun-dappled water, but a more common sight is an electric-blue dragonfly or a busy black and white water shrew. Sadly, the otter, which used to gamble and dive in the fast-flowing stream, has not been seen for several years. Many of the rivers and streams of the Devon and Cornwall coast have lost this animal through the continued practice of over-enthusiastic and cruel hunting.

Even the dead and dying trees support life. Holes drilled by woodpeckers are eagerly invaded by nesting birds and dead bark is home to a multitude of insects. However stunted, the trees themselves can offer protection to newly-planted firs and saplings; and when their useful life is over, fungi will consume the discarded decaying wood.

Late on a summer evening, the trail is alive with a different set of noises as nocturnal animals begin to stir. Dogfoxes jog through the woods, bats circle in the shell-pink sky and a tawny owl sets forth for a night's hunting.

Coombe Valley trail is close to both Bude and Kilkhampton, where there are sea and country campsites, and a variety of pursuits to enjoy. Apart from enjoying the sea from an exhilarating surfboard, there is sunbathing and walking along the miles of sand that skirt the waves – and the possibility of seeing a whiskery seal. Fishermen cast into the surf for bass from Summerleaze Beach, Crooklets Beach and Widemouth Bay; or take a boat into Bude Bay for cod, flounder or mackerel.

The sea washes over a swimming pool on the beach, tiny caves under the cliffs and the strands of rock-pools. Beachcombing is one of the most absorbing pastimes around Bude. More active exercise can be taken high above the sands on the breezy links of the Bude and North Cornwall golf course. Bude can also cater for the squash, tennis and bowls player, and there is a cinema and a museum for those inevitable wet days.

Gourmets have the best of both worlds, for the Devon border is just a stone's throw away. Your cream teas can either be served with thick-crusted and deep yellow Cornish cream, or the fluffy and white Devon variety.

Apart from nature trails such as Coombe Valley, there are outcrops of National Trust headland along the north coast.

Angling
Bude: several good spots for bass plus cod, flounder, mackerel & wrasse
Tackle shop: Wey's, 40 Queen Street
Tel: (0288) 2362
Bude Canal: coarse fishing with good access
Daily tickets: Bude Angling Association (D Allen), 10 Fairholme Road
River Tamar: major game river with fair access for visitors
Daily tickets: C & M Tidball, 20 The Square, Holsworthy
Tel: (0409) 253489
Water Authority: SWWA, 3–5 Barnfield Road, Exeter
Tel: (0392) 31666

Camping
Bude: Bude Holiday Park ►►►
Tel: (0288) 2472
Gently sloping 300-pitch site
Open Jun–Sep, no bookings
Wooda Farm Camping & Caravanning Park ►►
Tel: (0288) 2069
200-pitch site near sea
Open Apr–Aug, no bookings
Kilhampton: Easthorn Caravan & Camping Park ►►
Tel: (0288) 882) 235
Rural 19-pitch site
Open Apr–Oct, must book
Poundstock: Middle Penlean Caravan Site ►►
Tel: (028 885) 380
65-pitch site 10m S of Bude off A39

Open Apr–Oct must book Jul–Aug

Golfing
Bude & North Cornwall:
Tel: (0288) 2006
Well-kept links course, 18 holes, 6202yds, par 71, SSS70
Holsworthy:
Tel: (0409) 253177
Parkland course, 9 holes, 5808yds, par 70, SSS68

General
Boscastle: Museum of Witchcraft & Black Magic: fascinating collection of the occult
Open Easter–mid-Oct daily 10–7
Bude: Ebbingford Manor: Interesting mediaeval house
Open Jun–mid-Sep, Tue, Wed & Thu (plus Sun from Jul)
Launceston: Launceston Castle: ruins of 12th/13th-century fortress
Accessible all year
Shebbear: Alscott Farm Agricultural Museum: fascinating collection of vintage farm implements plus scale model exhibits, 9m S of Torrington off A388
Open Easter–Sep daily
Tel: (040 928) 206
Thornbury: Devon Museum of Mechanical Music: varied collection of early musical instruments, 5m NE of Holsworthy off A388
Open Easter–Oct daily 2–5
Tel: (040 926) 378

Cardinham Woods Trails

Forestry Commission, Dunmere, Bodmin, Cornwall
Tel: Bodmin (0208) 2577

> 2 miles east of Bodmin off unclassified road at Turfdown ¾ mile from A38
>
> Map reference: SX099667
>
> Four trails with themes: Riverside Walk – 1½ miles; Bluebell Walk – 2-mile extension of Riverside Walk taking in bluebell glades; Panorama Walk – 2½ miles (also connected to Bluebell Walk) with some steep sections; Silvermine Trail – 1½-mile extension of Riverside Walk with trip to Hurtstocks lead and silver mine
>
> *Facilities:* Illustrated trail guide from Forestry Commission and local tourist offices; car park, picnic area

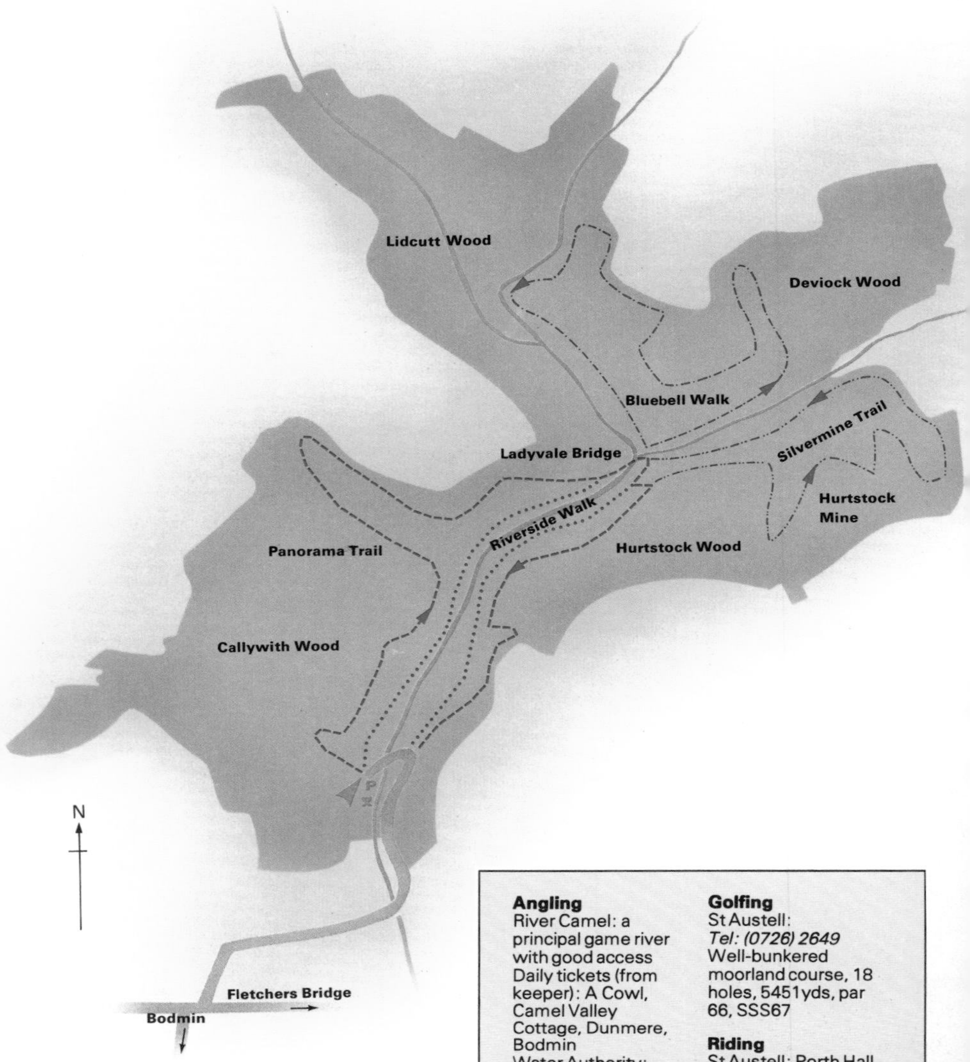

At the turn of the century, visitors to Cardinham Woods, tucked away on the edge of Bodmin Moor, were few and far between; the odd tinker or traveller, villagers searching for firewood and the passing poacher came and went and the local wildlife had free run of the valley. However, in the Thirties, the vale had a change of destiny when the Forestry Commission acquired the land from the estates of two neighbouring Lords.

At that time the woods were entirely oak coppice and during the next five years the unemployed of Bodmin – some thirty or so men – were set to work clearing the land and replanting it with conifers. A variety of species were chosen, including Douglas fir, Japanese larch, Sitka and Norwegian spruce, hemlock and the better-known Scots and Corsican pine. This latter variety, ranging in colour from dark, bluish-green through silvery grey to yellowish-green, ensures that the valley always looks attractive and that the overall appearance varies according to the season. The woods are a pleasant contrast to the stark moor.

In this country, a conifer will take about fifty years to reach maturity and consequently many of the trees at Cardinham have reached an ideal stage for felling. However, the Commission are exercising a policy whereby some trees are thinned out after twenty years onwards and others are allowed to continue growth, so avoiding wholesale clearance and allowing visitors the chance to observe the conifers throughout all stages of their growth.

To visit Cardinham Woods, take the A38 towards Plymouth and follow the road to Cardinham village. After half a mile, turn left and the road leads to the southern edge of the forest and to adequate parking facilities. Here the Forestry Commission have erected a series of picnic tables and benches which have been hewn from local timber for visitors' use.

Parties with elderly members in their midst should also note that seats have been constructed at regular intervals along the route of the Riverside Walk.

In the car park, a large noticeboard lists and colour codes the four way-marked walks that the Commission have recently established. These range from a mile to three-and-a-half miles in length and cover a variety of terrains and gradients.

The shortest trail – just a mile – back-tracks along the course of the stream into the heart of Callywith Wood and follows the route of the Commission's own roads. It is a level walk on firm paths that provides an opportunity to observe the variety of plant and wildlife that develops alongside a woodland stream. At the halfway mark, the path crosses the stream and heads back along the opposite bank in the direction of the car park.

The stone, boulder-built bridge that fords the stream, once served the former Chapel of our Lady of the Vale. The Chapel no longer stands and legend has it that the bridge was constructed from stones taken from the ruins. From the bridge, visitors can strike out in a choice of directions and follow either the Bluebell or Silvermine trails.

Bear left from the bridge and follow the steep path through the beech and Norway spruce of Callabarrett Wood to the top of the plateau. In late April to May the forest floor is a riot of bluebells – their bright blue heads

Angling
River Camel: a principal game river with good access
Daily tickets (from keeper): A Cowl, Camel Valley Cottage, Dunmere, Bodmin
Water Authority: SWWA, 3–5 Barnfield Road, Exeter
Tel: (0392) 31666
River Fowey: excellent sea trout fishing
Daily tickets & Water Authority: as River Camel

Camping
Bodmin: Camping Club Site ►
Tel: (0208) 3834
Undulating 200-pitch site
Open Apr–Sep, must book Jul–Aug
Lostwithiel: Downend Camp Site ►
Tel: (0208) 872363
Level 26-pitch site (6 tents)
Open May–Sep, must book Aug
Ruthernbridge: Ruthern Valley Holidays ►►►
Tel: (020 883) 395
Gently sloping 30-pitch site 2m SW of Bodmin off A30
Open May–Sep, must book
St Mabyn: Glenmorris Caravan & Camping Park ►►►
Tel: (020 884) 236
Rural 150-pitch site
Open Apr–Oct, must book Jul–Aug

Golfing
St Austell:
Tel: (0726) 2649
Well-bunkered moorland course, 18 holes, 5451yds, par 66, SSS67

Riding
St Austell: Porth Hall Riding Centre, Sticker
Tel: (0276) 4103

General
Bodmin: Military Museum: relics & items of the Duke of Cornwall's Light Infantry
Open Apr–Feb Mon–Fri
Pencarrow House: impressive Georgian mansion 3m NW of Bodmin
Open Easter–Sep (ex mon & Sat)
Tel: (020 884) 369
Lostwithiel: Lanhydrock: restored 17th-century house in wooded surroundings 3m N of Lostwithiel off B3268
Open Apr–Sep daily 11–6
Restormel Castle: mediaeval stronghold with notable keep 1m N of Lostwithiel off A390
Open all year
St Neot: Carnglaze Slate Caverns: guided tours round early slate mine
Open Easter–Sep times vary
Tel: (0579) 20251
Wadebridge: Hustyn Mill: design & craft centre
Open most times
Tel: (020 881) 2540

contrasting vividly with the sharp green spring foliage of the beech. Looking down through the valley from the plateau on a clear day it is possible to see the china clay mine tips in and around St Austell.

This area of Cornwall has strong mining traditions; tin, copper, silver and lead were mined extensively in the 18th- and 19th-centuries. Striking east from the bridge, the trail passes close to the ivy-clad ruins of Hurstocks Mine. These ruins are now unsafe and are fenced off from the public, however it is still possible to peer down into the open pit – often partially flooded – and appreciate the appalling and hazardous conditions in which the miners dug for lead and silver during the last century.

As a monument to the mining industry of the area, the Wheal Martyn Museum has been opened just north of St Austell. Here the clay workings, settling tanks, water wheels, wagons and potteries have been preserved for visitors.

The fourth trail, through the section of the plantation known as Callywith Wood, should take walkers a good two hours to complete and, although in places the paths are steep and slippery and several of the inclines may prove strenuous, the view down the valley towards the junction of the Glynn with the Fowey is truly rewarding.

In its early stages, the trail passes through a grove of oak trees. Due to the soil and climatic conditions typical to Cornwall, the oak has never fully developed and remains a relatively small and twisted tree. Although these trees are visually appealing, the timber is of little value commercially.

On the boundary of the woods, a belt of oak coppice has been preserved as a monument to former forest practices. Cropping the coppice once provided firewood and charcoal and supplied the local tanneries with bark for dying the leather. Although one such tannery remains at Grampound, it has now to rely on imported acorns for tanning.

Casual visitors to Cardinham may not catch a glimpse of the forest's wildlife while walking the trails, but naturalists who have set up observation points have been rewarded with sightings of rabbit, fox, hare and the irksome mink. Red and fallow deer do occasionally visit the woods, but these visits usually coincide with bad weather when the deer are forced from the open moor to find shelter elsewhere.

Just the other side of the A38 are the extensive grounds and woodlands of the Victorian mansion, Lanhydrock House. The paths through the 400-acre estate are open to the public and are at their best in May when there are magnificent displays of colourful shrubs such as rhododendrons and azaleas.

From the grounds of Lanhydrock, a footpath leads to the nearby ruins of Restormel Castle. A walled walk now encircles the site of the 12th-century castle and from this vantage point the River Fowey can clearly be seen.

The Fowey rises deep in the heart of Bodmin Moor and is renowned for salmon and more especially sea trout, while to the north, the Camel river is one of Cornwall's principal game rivers which can be prolific with salmon during the autumn months. Harbour fishing in

the Fowey is permitted as far as Lostwithiel and beach fishing from the town of Fowey itself.

Golfing enthusiasts should choose to travel either north or south for a day's play. At St Austell, the clifftop, championship course at Carlyon Bay welcomes visitors and to the north, at St Enodoc, is the highly acclaimed seaside course amongst the dunes and flats.

For overnight stays in the Cardinham area there are campsites at Ruthernbridge, St Mabyn, Lostwithiel and Lanlivery or, should you prefer a coastal setting, at Padstow, Tintagel, St Austell or Fowey.

Additional Forestry Commission trails can be enjoyed at Tregirls and Shortlanesend or alternatively it is possible to pick up the Peninsula Coastal Path at any number of points between Minehead and Poole.

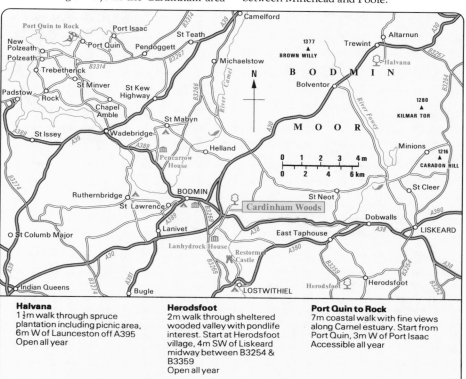

Halvana
1½m walk through spruce plantation including picnic area, 6m W of Launceston off A395 Open all year

Herodsfoot
2m walk through sheltered wooded valley with pondlife interest. Start at Herodsfoot village, 4m SW of Liskeard midway between B3254 & B3359 Open all year

Port Quin to Rock
7m coastal walk with fine views along Camel estuary. Start from Port Quin, 3m W of Port Isaac Accessible all year

Salcombe Hill Trail, Sidmouth

The Devon Trust for Nature Conservation, 2 Pennsylvania Road, Exeter
Tel: Exeter (0392) 79244

1½ miles off A3052 through Salcombe Regis or ¾ mile east of Sidmouth on unclassified road to Salcombe Regis

Map Reference: SY139882

4½-mile circuit of public footpaths crossing 500ft Salcombe Hill through trees and heath with beautiful sea views

Facilities: Information boards; illustrated brochure from local tourist information offices or from Devon Trust. Car Park at trail start

To the west of Lyme Bay, the National Trust has secured some five hundred acres of the lovely Devon coastline between Sidmouth and Branscombe. Adjacent to the western end of this strip of land, the Devon Trust has designed and maintains the Salcombe Hill Nature Trail. Although the inadequate coast road is constantly overcrowded during the summer months, you will find that the trail itself is visited by manageable numbers.

The walkway is situated on a plateau consisting of greensand upon marl, geologically similar to many spots in the south east Devon area. Holding no agricultural potential, this land was planted last century with broad-leaved woodland and, more recently, conifers.

From its start point at the car park off the Sidmouth-Salcombe Regis road, the trail follows a well-signposted four-and-a-half-mile circuit. The first section of the pathway has to be regularly cut back, to prevent the encroachment of the abundant gorse, bramble and bracken. The resultant dense thickets provide ample cover for tiny songbirds such as the wren and yellowhammer.

Turning westward, the trail now enters woodland. Mature oak and ash are prominent, but sweet chestnut and sycamore are also in evidence. You may be fortunate enough to spot a pair of buzzards who maintain a sporadic tenancy high up in a Scots pine, and spring walkers will most likely hear the chiffchaff's distinctive droning song, as the profuse insect life here makes migration unnecessary.

Over a stile and across the road is a second copse. Here the Scots pine and holm oak, interspersed by sycamore, enshroud the closely-grouped ivy and bramble bushes. You are sure to come across many fallen trees, ideal breeding grounds for many interesting fungal growths. Towards the next clearing, the natural muddiness of the path often betrays the passing of roe deer. However, daytime appearances of these elegant creatures are rare.

From this point of the trail, vegetation becomes markedly different. For you are now in the Observatory Estate, grounds in which the late Sir Norman and Lady Lockyer carried out extensive ornamental planting. The rhododendrons, daffodils and seventy-year-old cypresses are particularly impressive. A long-established sett is at the end of a tell-tale badger track near the estate's flint boundary wall. Full marks must go to the Devon Trust for enabling this burrower to thrive in what would otherwise be a hostile environment.

Beyond this wall the track meanders through a larch spinney to a point where steep steps are cut into the hillside allowing access down to Milltown Lane. The tall trees of this section are frequented by sparrow-hawks and carrion crows. If you notice movements in a heavily-foliaged nest at a trunk's main fork, the chances are that a grey squirrel family is in residence.

The track now climbs sharply up the heather-rich Soldier's Hill, affording a fine view of the Sid valley region. From the field at

the end of the now-wider track, you can glance down at the various domes and buildings of the Observatory Estate. The enterprising Sir Norman Lockyer had this private astronomical station built in 1912 when in his seventy-eighth year. Its present-day functions include study of upper atmosphere ionisation and environmental research. An annual open day is held during the summer, when the public can see for themselves the work carried out here.

Back across the road, the Forestry Commission has had the thick gorseland cleared and planted Norway Spruce and Douglas Fir. This was back in 1960, and although growth tends to be slow because of the exposed location, the trees have already changed this area.

Just beyond here, there is a short-cut back to the car park, but this means missing the sea views. Once past the large hunk of hard sandstone known as the Frog Stone, incoming waves can be heard crashing against the rocks five hundred feet below. Weather permitting, Berry Head, Brixham and Portland Bill (landmarks seventy miles apart) are both visible from the clifftop. Focus your eyes on the much nearer Beer Head and you will see several columns and pinnacles of composite white chalk, the result of a momentous ten-acre landslide two hundred years ago. The whole of the Sidmouth-Beer stretch of coast, on which you stand, is riddled with smugglers' caves, a legacy of the region's illegal 18th-century trade. Whitethroats, bullfinches and collared doves now patrol this area with endless swoops and dives.

On leaving the cliff's edge, the trail leads straight back to the parking lot. There is only space here for about thirty cars, but for some distance either side of the pull-in you can park safely on the verges. If by this time you have worked up an appetite, it is only a very short

Angling	
River Otter: mainly trout plus good mullet in estuary. Free fishing at Budleigh Salterton Water Authority: SWWA, 3–5 Barnfield Road, Exeter *Tel: (0392) 31666* Squabmoor Reservoir: stillwater offering mixed fishing at Budleigh Salterton Daily tickets (in advance): Knowle Post Office, 2m E of Budleigh Salterton. No licence required	SSS69 Honiton: *Tel: (0404) 2943* Easily walked parkland course, 18 holes, 5239yds, par 67, SSS66 Sidmouth: *Tel: (039 55) 3023* Scenic hillside course, 18 holes, 5188yds, par 66, SSS65
Camping	**General**
Salcombe Regis: Kings Down Tail Caravan & Camping Site ► *Tel: (029 780) 313* Level 100-pitch site Open mid-Mar–mid-Nov, must book Jul–Aug Salcombe Regis Caravan & Camping Site ►► *Tel: (039 55) 4303* 100-pitch (40 caravans) hilltop site Open Apr–Sep, must book Jul–Aug Sidmouth: Ladram Bay Caravan Site ► *Tel: (0395) 68398* Large 272-pitch site (22 caravans) Open May–Sep, no bookings Weston: Oakdown Touring Caravan Park ►►► *Tel: (029 780) 387* Level 52-pitch site (6 tents) 4m E of Sidmouth Open mid-Mar–Nov, must book Jul–Aug	Beer: Beer Heights Light Railway: steam-operated passenger line with scenic views across Seaton Bay Open May–mid-Oct Mon–Fri & Sat mornings *Tel: (0297) 21542 ext 36* Budleigh Salterton: Fairlynch Arts Centre & Museum: local exhibits plus costume display Open Easter–Oct 2.30–5 (ex Sun), plus mornings Jul–Aug *Tel: (039 54) 2666* Honiton: Allhallows Museum: lace displays plus historical documents Open May–Sep daily 10–5 *Tel: (040 487) 307* Otterton: Otterton Mill: ancient working cornmill plus craft workshops Open Easter–Sep daily 2–5.30 (workshops open all year) *Tel: (0395) 68521* Ottery St Mary: Cadhay: fine 16th-century house Open mid-Jul–Aug Wed & Thu *Tel: (040 481) 2432* Sidmouth: Sidmouth Museum: varied collection in fine Georgian house Open Easter then May–Sep daily (ex Sun mornings) *Tel: (039 55) 2357/2946*
Golfing	
Budleigh Salterton: East Devon: *Tel: (039 54) 2018* Downland/heather course 1m W of Budleigh Salterton off A376, 18 holes, 6140yds, par 70,	

Sidmouth and Beer Head from Peak Hill

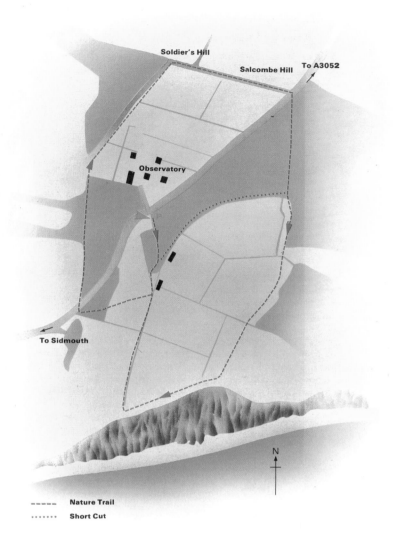

Soldier's Hill

Salcombe Hill   To A3052

Observatory

To Sidmouth

N

----- Nature Trail

······ Short Cut

walk to a delightful 12th-century church, near which is an old-world shop serving traditional Devonshire cream teas.

Away from here, ardent trail-tracers have dozens to choose from at Farway Countryside Park near Honiton. Also within these hundred-and-thirty-acre grounds pony and donkey-cart rides may be taken and the children will love to see all the farm animals roving about at will.

In Honiton itself, there is a pleasant parkland golf course which welcomes visitors and the progress of the town's internationally-famous lace-making industry is traced by clever displays at the Allhallows Museum.

At the resort of Beer, a passenger train plies the scenic route beside the bay to the sure delight of all steam railway enthusiasts. The track also passes through the fun-filled Peko Pleasure Park.

In the village of Branscombe there is a tiny bakery which, amazingly, still produces bread from ovens fired by wood faggots. Several miles of footpath connect Branscombe with Lincombe and Western Combe, providing walkers with more clifftop vistas. Branscombe is particulary fascinating since it has rich red cliffs to the south and slate grey cliffs to the north.

Back westward, near to the large Ladram Bay Caravan Site, is the tiny village of Otterton where a cornmill mentioned in the Doomsday Book has been lovingly restored. Various craft items are made and sold at the adjacent workshops. From Otterton you can go down to the sea again, via the estuary of the River Otter. Anglers will appreciate the free fishing for trout and mullet at Budleigh Salterton where the estuary meets Ladram Bay.

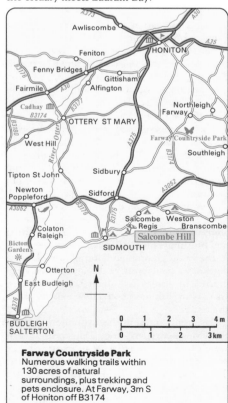

Farway Countryside Park
Numerous walking trails within 130 acres of natural surroundings, plus trekking and pets enclosure. At Farway, 3m S of Honiton off B3174

Dunsford Nature Reserve

The Devon Trust for Nature Conservation, 2 Pennsylvania Road, Exeter
Tel: Exeter (0392) 79244

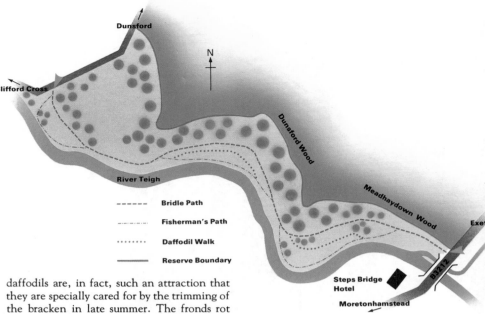

- – – – – – Bridle Path
- – · – · – · Fisherman's Path
- · · · · · · · Daffodil Walk
- ———— Reserve Boundary

On B3212 south west of Dunsford village and 9 miles from Exeter

Map reference: SX805884

2-mile long Reserve with bridle path, Fisherman's Path, and Daffodil Walk in wooded river valley

Facilities: Information board at trail entrances; illustrated brochure from tourist information caravan on B3212 (about 250 yards east of trail entrance) or from Devon Trust, Steps Bridge Hotel, 100yds from trail entrance

There is many a holiday-maker stuck in the bumper-to-bumper drudgery of the A38 in high summer who must wonder if there is not an alternative route to the delights of Cornwall. There is, of course, but the B3212, carving its way across the heart of Dartmoor from Exeter to Yelverton deserves more than a transitory glance. While the moors can be enjoyed through the windscreen, the surprisingly varied vegetation and animal life of this area of Devon can only be fully appreciated on foot.

Over the years, numerous Dartmoor walkways have been designated and run by enterprising conservation groups, and the trail near Dunsford, developed by the Devon Trust for Nature Conservation, is a fine example. The trail, situated in a 140-acre Nature Reserve on the steep valley side of the Teign, is in the north-eastern corner of the Dartmoor National Park on the B3212 between Dunsford and Moretonhampstead.

The eastern end and normal start of the walk is Steps Bridge, a natural beauty spot rich in flora and fauna. The bridge itself, as the inscribed stones reveal, was built in 1816 and marks the boundary of Dunsford and Bridford parishes.

The nearby Steps Bridge Hotel has a self-service restaurant and a large beer-garden – ample parking space makes it an ideal starting and finishing point. Wild ducks and deer breed in the hotel grounds and during June the gardens have an impressive display of rhododendrons. In somewhat simpler surroundings, there is a youth hostel directly opposite, across the B3212.

The trail, running the two-mile length of the Meadhaydown and Dunsford Woods which form the Reserve, is an existing bridle path, with deviations down to the banks of the Teign and the valley floor area which is called the Fisherman's Path. Two short detours are named the Daffodil Walk for the sights they afford of this springtime delight. Dunsford's

daffodils are, in fact, such an attraction that they are specially cared for by the trimming of the bracken in late summer. The fronds rot away and the daffodils grow up unhindered in the following spring.

Much of the Reserve's woodland was coppiced for many years to provide the wood for fencing, charcoal and firewood. Dunsford has a rich mix of deciduous trees including oak (predominant), birch, beech, alder, ash and sycamore and these are cut back every twenty-five years or so to sprout and grow again. Just a few trees were allowed to develop to maturity to provide larger timbers. The Devon Trust has now re-introduced coppicing to restore the woodland to the natural status it would have enjoyed for centuries. Good coppice management keeps clearings open from the encroachment of blackthorn, provides abundant material for the support of fungi and enables birds, insects and small mammals to colonise the stacks of cut wood.

Of course, it is the River Teign, forming the Reserve's south boundary that dominates the environment. Flowing over the Carboniferous slates, shales and sandstone inclusions which characterise the Dartmoor fringe, the Teign has shed its load of loam over the water-borne gravel of the valley floor. It is in these damp conditions that mosses, lichens and fungi survive and thrive and the Trust is encouraging this aspect of the Reserve's flora actively.

Angling
Meldon: fly fishing for trout at Okehampton
Daily tickets : on-site ticket machine. No licence required
River Teign: good game river, at its best in Spring
Daily tickets (in advance): J Bowden & Son, The Square, Chagford
Tel: (064 73) 3271
Water Authority: SWWA, 3–5 Barnfield Road, Exeter
Tel: (0392) 31666

Camping
Chudleigh Knighton: Ford Farm ▶
Tel: (0626) 853253
Small 48-pitch site (18 caravans)
Open Mar–Oct, must book for caravans
Moretonhampstead: Clifford Bridge Caravan Park ▶▶▶
Tel: (064 724) 226
Grassy 20-pitch site (no tents) 3m NE of Moretonhampstead off B3212
Open mid-Mar–Oct, must book Jul–Aug
Whiddon Down: Martin Farm Caravan & Camping Site ▶
Tel: (064 723) 202
Level 40-pitch site 8m E of Okehampton off A30
Open Easter–Sep, must book Jul–Aug

Golfing
Moretonhampstead: Manor House Hotel:
Tel: (064 74) 355
Pleasant parkland course 1m E of Moretonhampstead off B3212, 18 holes,

6016yds, par 69, SSS69
Okehampton:
Tel: (0837) 2113
Appealing moorland course, 18 holes, 5251yds, par 68, SSS66

Riding
Newton Abbot: Pinchaford Riding Centre (J R Shelton), Haytor
Tel: (036 46) 251

General
Ashburton: Ashburton Museum: local antiquities, geology & weaponry
Open May–Sep, Tue, Thu, Fri & Sat afternoons
Tel: (0364) 52298
Drewsteignton: Castle Drogo: modern granite castle off A382 at Sandy Park
Open Apr–Oct daily 11–6
Newton Abbot: New Devon Pottery: pottery & leather workshops plus picnic area
Open Easter–Oct daily (ex Sat & Sun)
Tel: (0626) 4262
Okehampton: Okehampton Castle: 11th–14th-century fortress
Open all year
Sticklepath: Museum of Rural Industry: converted mills housing agricultural machinery, 4m E of Okehampton off A30
Open all year daily 11–6
Tel: (083 784) 286/352

Lydford Gorge

Snowdrops are another valley-floor resident which, it is hoped, will spread throughout the bank area. Marsh plants are found in profusion including marigold, meadow sweet, and the tall grooved stems of the poisonous hemlock, water dropwort.

Fishing on this part of the Teign is private but in a few quiet minutes spent on the bank you should see the brown trout holding its station, nose to the current and waiting for insect larvae and pupae to float into its orbit. The Teign has a fairly healthy autumn and spring salmon run, with migratory trout appearing in the late spring and summer. The Teign was unlucky enough to have the first known wild colony of the voracious mink, breeding from escaped mink farm animals – they are occasionally sighted in the Reserve. Otters might be present under the banks, too, but this rare and endangered water mammal has not been seen recently and the Trust ask visitors to report on sightings.

While keen entomologists will find that the weir at Steps Bridge is an ideal place to spot the many aquatic insects of the Teign, including may-flies and the pond-skater, Dunsford is not a great haven of insects due to the very dense nature of the woods and ground cover. There are some unusual colonies of wood crickets, said to be the highest and furthest inland in the county, and some twenty-six species of butterfly are recorded. Britain's largest ant species, the wood ant which is about half an inch long, is living throughout the woods, the most immediate sign of its presence being the characteristic three-inch high mound, capped by woodland debris, which is just the iceberg tip of the underground colony.

Dunsford has a typical population of woodland birds, including the wood warbler, missel thrush, five species of tits and three woodpeckers, including the rare lesser spotted species. You will really have to wait a considerable time to see these species against the wood's dark

backdrop. On the lighter fringes and gorse-speckled uplands of the Reserve's west end (towards Clifford Cross) there is more bird song and summer visitors make their home – the rare grasshopper warbler has been seen here. Down by the river, an occasional heron feeds and you may just glimpse the blue flash of the kingfisher.

Fallow deer are very shy but they are present at Dunsford, their tracks being visible throughout the woods. They may be seen on the higher ground of the Reserve.

The walk at Dunsford taking the Fisherman's Path and the bridle path is a maximum of four-and-a-quarter miles – or some two-and-a-half hours at a leisurely amble. There is access from the Clifford Bridge end of the Reserve close to an attractive moorland caravan site, one of many opportunities for outdoor living in the area.

While the Reserve's waters are private, fishing the Teign is possible – enquire at J Bowdon & Son in nearby Chagford. If you would like a round or two of golf, the famous Manor House Hotel course is some five miles away to the south west of Moretonhampstead. Here the

River Bovey is the major hazard, on a course made famous by Peter Alliss's television series of instruction.

If after all this ruralism you care for a glimpse of city life, then Exeter is only nine miles away. Among the city's many sights are the Maritime Museum, a very early Guildhall, the lovely cathedral and an underground labyrinth of mediaeval aqueducts which once supplied the city water. In the Drewsteignton area, Castle Drogo is a major attraction. It is a granite extravaganza which is possibly the last grand-scale country house to be built in Britain – it was designed by Edward Lutyens early this century. More Dartmoor granite can be seen in the nearby 400-year-old Fingle Bridge. Further downstream, overlooking the Teign is Prestonbury Castle, the earthwork ramparts of an Iron Age fort.

Dunsford is not the only reserve in this region of the Dartmoor fringe – Yarner Wood National Nature Reserve is of particular interest to bird-watchers. More energetic walkers may like to tackle the heights of the Fernworthy Forest Trail which climbs four miles over tors, reaching over 1600 feet.

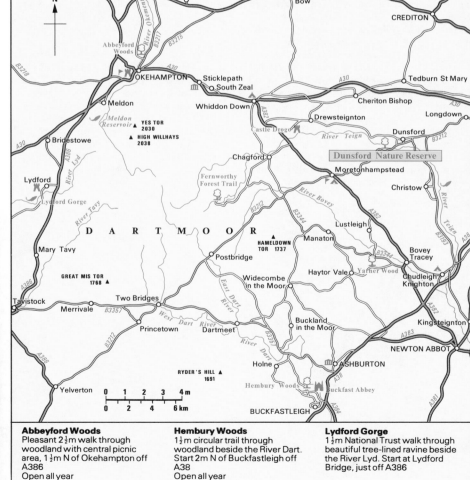

Abbeyford Woods
Pleasant 2½m walk through woodland with central picnic area, 1½m N of Okehampton off A386
Open all year

Fernworthy Forest Trail
Hilly 4m walk within Dartmoor National Park, 6m W of Moretonhampstead off B3212
Open all year

Hembury Woods
1½m circular trail through woodland beside the River Dart. Start 2m N of Buckfastleigh off A38
Open all year

Lydford Gorge
1½m National Trust walk through beautiful tree-lined ravine beside the River Lyd. Start at Lydford Bridge, just off A386

Yarner Wood National Nature Reserve
3½m marked walk through trees, rich in birds. Start at lodge 4m NW of Bovey Tracey off B3344

Kennet and Avon Canal Walk

Department of Leisure and Tourist Service, Bath City Council, The Pump Room, Stall Street, Bath
Tel: Bath (0225) 61111

From station go under railway and over the Avon – turn left into Claverton Street and left again. The first canal lock is off Spring Gardens Road

Map reference: ST755643

2-mile urban and suburban canal walk with features of both industrial and natural history interest

Facilities: Illustrated trail brochure from tourist and city council offices (also a Heritage Trail); three car parks within easy walking distance

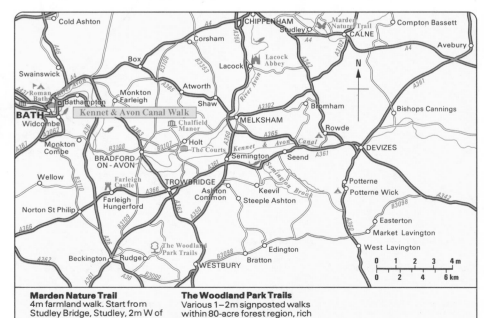

It probably comes as some surprise to learn that the art of building canals and river navigations stretches back to Roman times. But it was not until the early 18th century that waterways began to make an economic impact on the transport of minerals, industrial goods and agricultural produce. It was in this first flush of the Canal Age that the waters of what was to become the Kennet and Avon Canal began to reach out towards one another across Wiltshire and Berkshire. The Kennet from Reading to Newbury was navigable in 1727 and, at the other end, the Avon river was opened up to Bath four years later. It was not until 1810 that these two rivers were actually joined by the canal between the centre of Bath and Newbury. The complete length, which has over one hundred locks, is eighty-six miles, of which some are now navigable again after restoration by the Kennet and Avon Canal Trust in conjunction with the British Waterways Board and other conservation groups. By the mid-Eighties, the whole canal will be opened to pleasure craft.

Along the first section of the artificial waterway completed by engineer John Rennie in 1804, Bath City Council has arranged a most unusual canalside nature trail which is also the route of a slightly shorter Heritage Trail. Starting from the point at which the navigation joins the Avon, the nature trail follows the tow-path for two miles to the village of Bathampton. You will find the start of the trail at Lock 7 in Spring Gardens Road, close to the main railway station.

The canal rises near Bath itself through a set of six locks (called the Widcombe Flight) interspersed with boat-loading basins and compensating ponds which provide the canal with water to make up the loss through the lock

Angling
River Avon: recently re-stocked with barbel towards Bath, but visitors' chances limited
Daily tickets: Bath Angling Association (A J Smith), 30 Charles Street, Bath
Water Authority: WWA, Techno House, Redcliffe Way, Bristol
Tel: (0272) 25462/ 25491
Semington Brook: good mixed fishing 3m S of Devizes to Holt
Daily tickets: Lavington Angling Club (M Gilbert), Gable Cottage, 24 High Street, Erlestoke, Devizes
Tel: (038 083) 425

Camping
Bath: Newbridge Caravan Park ►►►►
Tel: (0225) 28778
Small 72-pitch site Open all year, must book Jul–Aug
Potterne: Potterne Wick Touring Caravan Park ►►►
Tel: (0380) 3277
Grassy 30-pitch site 2m S of Devizes Open Apr–Oct, must book Jul–Aug
Rowde: Lakeside:
Tel: (0380) 2767
Level 30-pitch site 2m NW of Devizes Open Apr–Oct, must book

Golfing
Bath:
Tel: (0225) 5334
Interesting upland course, 18 holes, 6328yds, par 70, SSS70

West Wiltshire (Warminster):
Tel: (0985) 2110
Windswept hilltop course, 18 holes, 5732yds, par 70, SSS68

General
Bath: Bath Carriage Museum: largest collection of horse-drawn carriages in England
Open all year
Tel: (0225) 25175
Museum of Costume: huge clothing & fashion display plus toys & dolls, housed in the Assembly Rooms
Open all year
Tel: (0225) 61111 ext 324
Roman Baths & Pump Room: remains of Roman bathing complex including hot water spring
Open all year
Tel: as Museum of Costume
Bradford on Avon: Barton Tithe Barn: 168ft-long 14th-century barn. Accessible at all times
Great Chalfield Manor: restored 15th-century mansion
Open mid-Apr–Sep (Wed only)
Holt: The Courts: late 17th-century house with topiary tree-gardens
Open Apr–Oct 2–6.30 (ex Sat & Sun)
Trowbridge: Farleigh Castle: 14th-century fortress remains 4m W of Trowbridge off A366
Open all year

Marden Nature Trail
4m farmland walk. Start from Studley Bridge, Studley, 2m W of Calne
Open Apr–Sep

The Woodland Park Trails
Various 1–2m signposted walks within 80-acre forest region, rich in plant and bird life. Start from Brokerswood, Rudge 3m W of Westbury off A36
Open all year

Clapham Wharf, Kennet and Avon Canal

under them are moorhens. This unusual bird will nest on the water, on the bank or even in trees and bushes along the tow-path.

Trees that make their appearance in hedges along the tow-path and at the water's edge are the crack willow, ash, hawthorn, cherry, horse chestnut, silver birch and pear – quite a variety within a stone's throw of a busy city centre. You may see two types of lily in the canal's larger pools. The smaller yellow flowers of *Nuphar lutea* (sometimes called brandybottle) can appear as early as June, while the white bowls of *Nymphaea alba* appear in July and August. Behind Horseshoe Pond is a fine decorated stone chimney – the remains of a pumping station once used to lift river water up to the higher basins.

By Lock 13 the canal has risen some fifty feet above the level of the Avon and there is a long straight stretch with views of the city centre from the land next to the tow-path, which has been landscaped with ash, silver birch and maple trees. A former malting building, complete with its kiln, has been renovated on the opposite bank. Swans make their appearance at this point and the first pair you come across may well be in the reeds opposite a handy seat by the lengthsman's cottage (he not only controlled the lock but also looked after the banks and tow-path of his 'length').

sometimes float through the air and the three-foot stems of loosestrife shows its ragged purple clusters. Right at the edge in the wet no-man's land are plants such as water forget-me-not.

Candy's Bridge, and the trail is drawing to a close with a final natural curiosity – the Turkey Oak, of which there are several examples in the clump of trees beyond the bridge. A member of the *Quercus* family, it grows much faster and so tends to become more dominant than a natural oak. You will recognise it by the furry and stalkless acorn cups.

Bathampton is the end of this organised part of the walk – although of course the tow-path goes on to the heights of the canal at the twenty-nine Caen Hill locks and on to Newbury.

You can walk back to Bath across Bathampton Meadows or take public transport. The city's Department of Architecture publishes a series of historic Heritage Trails which take the visitor around the sights of the town. Major

gates. Road construction lead to the demolition of Lock 8 and the deepening of Lock 9 which you may notice as you continue up the flight past the little iron Stothert and Pitt bridge to the first of the more open waters at Long Pond. The allotments on the ground opposite the tow-path are known to date back before the canal was opened and have the unusual name of Terrafirma. Here in Long Pond, and in nearby Horseshoe Pond, you may see water lilies. Darting between and diving

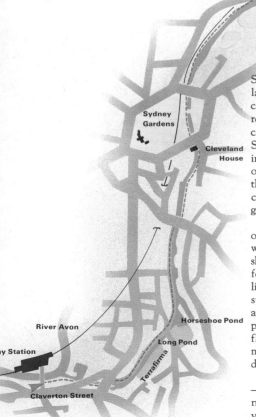

Before reaching one of Bath's many parks at Sydney Gardens, the canal passes under Cleveland House, former headquarters of the canal company, complete with a hole in the tunnel roof through which passing bargees could receive packages, letters and, no doubt, pay. Sydney Gardens features some superb trees, including an unusual hybrid plane which flakes off large quantities of bark. It is recorded that the former owners of the gardens charged the canal builders the small fortune of 2000 guineas for the right of way.

Increased boat traffic on the canal throughout this stretch is keeping both lilies and other water weeds at bay but the plant colonies of the shallower bankside water are an ideal habitat for both fish and the insects and simple aquatic life that they feed on. The canal, which is stocked with fish in some of its reaches, has always been a favourite for anglers. Common plants to be found in this canal fringe are the floating duck-weeds, water plantain, water mint, which lightly scents the air on summer days, and the tall stems of yellow flag iris.

There are wild flowers by the tow-path, too – the short twisted stems of the white dead nettle are more common than the stinging variety, rosebay willowherb seed parachutes

draws are, of course, the Pump Room and Roman Baths. Today's building is on the site of a temple to the goddess of the waters, Sulis Minerva, and excavations completed in 1979, while tracking down the source of a waterborne disease, revealed a rich store of Roman objects devoted to her.

An attraction is the Regency terraces of the father-and-son design team, John Wood Elder and Younger. The thirty houses of the Royal Crescent, the thirty-three houses of the Circus sharing over 600 Doric and Ionic columns between them and the Hot Bath are among their many works.

Further west from Bath, the Kennet and Avon canal runs through Bradford on Avon, a community that benefited from the prosperity of the wool trade like Bath. The two towns form an axis around which there is a cluster of stately homes and manors to visit. Within ten miles are Claverton Manor, Great Chalfield Manor, Farleigh Castle and Westwood Manor. Claverton Manor, which houses the American Museum in Britain, is particularly interesting – Winston Churchill delivered his first-ever political speech there in 1897.

If you are an outdoor-living enthusiast, Bath has two campsites on its outskirts at Newbridge and Corston Fields. If you fancy a round of golf, there are two fine 18-hole courses at Sham Castle and Lansdown Park.

Outside the city, many walkers will aim for the Mendips and the scenic grandeur of Cheddar Gorge. Here, around the head of the gorge, are a number of way-marked country trails that are a splendid antidote to the natural history of Bath's Kennet and Avon backwaters.

Bolderwood Forest Walks

Forestry Commission, The Queen's House, Lyndhurst, Hampshire SO4 7NH
Tel: Lyndhurst (042 128) 2801

On unclassified road 1 mile south east off A31 Southampton–Ringwood road, 6½ miles north east of Ringwood

Map reference: SZ243087

Three walks through a central New Forest highland among mature trees:
Radnor Walk – ¾ mile;
Arboretum Walk – 1¼ miles;
Mark Ash Walk – 3½ miles

Facilities: Trail notes or full guide book (*Explore the New Forest* HMSO); car parks; picnic areas

The New Forest is, of course, a complete misnomer. This 92 000-acre expanse of ancient woodlands, new plantations, cattle and horse pasture and heather-clad moors actually celebrated its nine-hundredth birthday in 1979. It is not essentially a true forest today because between the many dense stands of trees, equal areas of meadow and moor, busy villages, drives and roads interpose. Officially decreed a Royal hunting forest by William the Conqueror, perhaps the only thing that remains unchanged is that this vast area is a tremendous recreational amenity. Within the bounds of this twenty-mile belt are walks galore, beautiful camping grounds seemingly deep in the woods (in reality a stone's throw from the roads), fishing and pony-trekking opportunities.

In this concise look at the New Forest it is the trails and walks of the Bolderwood Grounds that are featured. Taking their name from that of the Master Keeper's Lodge demolished in 1833 (*bolder* is an old English word for a house) the three walks lace through some of the more mature woodlands of the New Forest which are of great scenic beauty and antiquity.

The walks, detailed in a trail brochure and in the official New Forest Guide, are a maze of paths colour-coded to keep ramblers on the straight and narrow. Shortest of all is the Radnor Walk, following yellow sign boards. A major feature of the trail is the stand of 120-year-old Douglas firs that once formed a large part of the Keeper's Lodge grounds. It is also worth taking for the sight you gain of the Radnor Stone.

Carved from delicately-shaded Westmorland slate in masonry workshops in Bournemouth, the Stone is a modern memorial to William, seventh Earl of Radnor, a chairman of the Forestry Commission and New Forest Verderer (the chief forest officer responsible for the well-being of the trees and deer-herds).

Carvings on the stone depict forest wildlife and the trees in great detail.

Even William the Conqueror is said to have disliked the New Forest's verderers for their strict laying down of the hunting law – but unlike William they survive to this day. The court of the verderers still meets every two months, electing three Agisters (responsible for livestock) and a Steward to police the forest, often on horseback, safeguarding the well-being of the animals. In addition, a team of keepers patrols individual forest preserves and enclosures, culling the deer where it seems necessary and keeping down other small mammals which damage the young trees.

Central on the Radnor Stone and undoubtedly one of the New Forest's most popular features, are the forest ponies. These sturdy, sure-footed animals wander throughout the forest singly and in herds, seemingly oblivious to the motor-car and the people who come to stare. All the horses are privately owned and branded with their owners' names – owners pay a fee to the Agisters for grazing within the forest. Strictly speaking, only registered stallions are allowed to serve New Forest mares to

A New Forest Glade

maintain the breed's individuality, but the odd horse of other breeds has got into the forest and there are some horses every year with something of a mixed parentage. The ponies are rounded up at various times of the year and official pony sales held near Beaulieu station have become a popular tourist attraction. Never feed New Forest ponies—not only can a diet of picnic leftovers upset them but they are completely wild and occasionally both playful or alternatively, vicious.

The Radnor Stone also depicts trees, of course. It is the oak that is the dominant tree of the New Forest's woodlands and principally the pedunculate species, *Quercus robur*. Enormous numbers of acorns fall to the ground across the forest and these are poisonous to the ponies while they are green. The answer to this is a process, which again has survived the centuries. Pigs are called in to snuffle around the forest floor eating up the acorns—this autumnal rite is called 'pannage'. Some pigs escape the swineherd's attention when being rounded up and there are a considerable number of wild pigs in the woods now.

Venison has been a prized meat for centuries

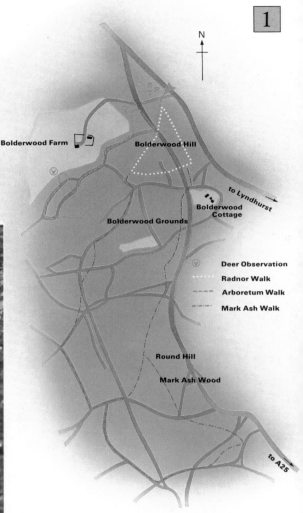

and it seems odd that at one time the majority of the New Forest deer were culled in an effort to wipe them out completely and make the forest a much more prolific wood-bearing area. Happily the attempt failed and the remaining individual animals were soon breeding again. It is the fallow deer that is the major species present but there are red, Sika and roe deer, too. The fine stag shown on the Radnor Stone has the magnificent antlers of a seven or eight-year-old fallow buck. Keeping the numbers down by culling and sale of the venison is good for the herds—one of the major reasons is to ensure that the herd size does not exceed the available food supply. If you want to sample the rich and fibrous meat, shops in Lyndhurst and other New Forest centres sell it all year round in a variety of products.

As you leave the Radnor Stone you will walk gently up Bolderwood Hill and see the smaller Douglas firs, trees that have regenerated naturally. Eventually they will be replanted to take the place of the older trees in the main stand, which are long past their prime growing age.

While on the first part of the Radnor Walk you are also on your way along the Mark Ash Walk—the longest of the Bolderwood trails. Follow the red markers and you will discover one of the oldest woodlands in the New Forest, its name taken from the form of the traditional boundaries to forest areas, a line of ash trees.

The early part of the walk is through the Oakley Inclosure, which is fenced or wired off to prevent the ingress of commoners' grazing cattle. It is a woodland of the future, as few of

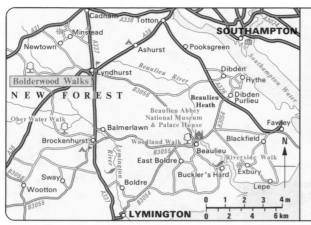

the trees have reached full maturity. Without nibbling cattle, a wide diversity of species will develop with a considerable span of ages. The oaks here have grown very tall and straight compared with the scattered trees one sees in meadows or wood fringes with more lighting.

The forest can at times seem alive with flowers. On the ground in the appropriate seasons are the white, blue and yellow spikes of wild garlic, bluebell and primrose—in the air you may see the pink and white candles of the occasional chestnut or the delicate splashes of wild cherry. Wild gladioli flower in summer, while the patches of marshier ground, soft and acid, bear marsh gentian and bog orchid. Amid the grasses, sedges, mosses and whortleberry, flutter bright butterflies and if you are lucky you may see a grass snake or common lizard basking in the sun. The adder is present in the New Forest and, in fact, there is here an all-black form of the normally black and green-patterned snake.

While the larger mammals are the most common sight in the Forest, the patient naturalist waiting until the evening could spot fox, badger, rabbit and hare. The predatory birds come out at this time too. The tawny and barn owls do not have the Forest's small mammals to themselves—there is a fairly rare summer visitor in the woods, the honey buzzard. Normally eating the grubs from bee and wasp nests, which it tears apart, it will take field mice, voles and lizards.

Mark Ash Wood, the destination of this walk, is one of the oldest parts of the forest and contains ancient beeches up to 260 years old. Beeches growing close together create an inhibiting factor in the soil which prevents natural regeneration around adult trees and this, coupled with the shade, means there are few younger trees in this part of the wood. The old trees are over-mature and will eventually have to be felled. In a few small groups, naturally regenerating trees have been fenced off from the attentions of grazing cattle and within the enclosures are beech, sallow and birch which will become the nucleus of new woods when the old trees are cleared. The path returns via Pound Hill and a view point.

In 1860 in the grounds of Bolderwood Manor, an arboretum was planted which now contains a magnificent display of over forty trees of thirty-five different species. Some of the trees are considered to be the finest examples of their species in Britain. A path leads from the Radnor Stone to the Arboretum Walk, or alternatively it can be reached by diverting from the Mark Ash trail.

Consisting of both ornamental and commercial species, the Arboretum trees are numbered and a full key is contained in the trail brochure. Among the special trees are a Californian Redwood (*Sequoia sempervirens*) about 120ft high, a *Wellingtonia* of about 150ft (it is a tree which can live to over 3000 years old in its home forests of California) and two Australian cider gums (the *Eucalyptus* on which koala bears feed).

Although the Arboretum receives the bulk of its visitors during the summer months, it is particularly attractive both as the leaves turn in the autumn and as the bright green, spring foliage bursts forth after the long winter.

For car-bound visitors, an ornamental drive has been established on the same route as the old horse-drawn carriages used to take through the Bolderwood section of the forest. However, the narrow road continues further south than the trails, through an ancient, pollarded grove and past the famous Knightwood Oak which is thought to have been planted in 1697.

Similarly, the Rhinefield Ornamental Drive and its associate walk, leads through a wide belt of conifers planted in 1859 in the grounds of Rhinefield House. There are over fifty trees to view and all are meticulously labelled with both their height and their girth recorded for posterity. The accompanying Tall Tree walk has been specifically laid out to accommodate both pushchairs and invalid chairs.

Naturalists may care to extend their travels in this area and follow the Brock Hill trail which culminates at a hillside badger sett, carefully monitored by the Forestry Commission to ensure the survival of the black and white 'brocks'.

Car parks are too numerous to mention and perfect picnic sites superlative, while for campers and caravanners the Forestry Commission have established several full facilities sites and a dozen sites designed for the purist, equipped with only the basic facilities necessary to enjoy a woodland holiday.

It is not only walkers and naturalists that may enjoy the forest: anglers may care to walk across Beaulieu Heath to Hatchett Pond for coarse fishing or visit the trout fisheries at Emery Down or try their hand at casting for carp at Minstead Mill Lake.

Golfers can visit the 18-hole woodland course close by at Brockenhurst Manor or venture further afield to Barton-on-Sea. Horse riding and pony trekking are well-catered for at the numerous local stables and, if watching rather than participating is your idea of sport, there is an old world village cricket green just outside Lyndhurst.

The ancient royal manor of Lyndhurst is the undisputed capital of the forest with its manor house and adjoining Verderers' Hall, thatched, timbered and brightly-painted houses.

The Beaulieu River meanders from the heart of Denny Lodge, a favourite haunt of roe deer, past the National Motor Museum and the ruins of the Cistercian monastery through the tourist-tired village and south towards the Solent. An oxbow in the river at Bucklers Hard provides the perfect harbour and shelters the boatyards where the ships of Nelson's fleet were once built from local oaks. The boatyards and cottages of the village have been sympathetically restored and now house a maritime museum recording this phase of Britain's great naval heritage.

Queen Elizabeth Country Park

Park Centre, Gravel Hill,
Horndean, Portsmouth,
Hampshire, PO8 0QE
Tel: Horndean (0705) 595040

On A3 between Petersfield (4 miles)
and Portsmouth (13 miles) – well-
signposted

Map reference: SU719183

Four trails covering different aspects of
wood and downland conservation area:
Centre Trail – 3½ miles; Holt Trail – 2½
miles; Butser Trail – 2½ miles; Tree Trail –
1½ miles (level, suitable for disabled
people)

Facilities: Illustrated trail brochures and
maps; several car parks; picnic areas;
exhibitions and displays in Park Centre;
ancient farm demonstration; regular
calendar of events

There is no mistaking the scenery of the South
Downs in Sussex. Broad sweeps of wooded
valleys and miles of rolling country, with flint-
faced cottages and rambling arable farms: tell-
tale characteristics of chalkland. This ridge of
hills, so beloved of walkers, rises humbly in the
east of Hampshire and ends in a spectacular
575ft drop of dazzling white rock at Beachy
Head.

Impressive though the South Downs are,
they lie fairly low on the skyline. Major sum-
mits are at Ditchling Beacon (813ft), Win-
dover Hill (707ft) and Firle Beacon (713ft).
Highest of all is Butser Hill, at almost 900ft,
which is part of Ramsdean Down and within
the boundaries of the Queen Elizabeth Country Park, south west of Petersfield.

The Park covers 1400 acres of downland and
mixed beech and coniferous woodland and is
administered jointly by the Forestry Commission and Hampshire County Council. Not surprisingly, the Park offers far more than an
enjoyable afternoon's walking. It would probably take a full day to sample all the attractions
which vary from hang gliding to an Iron Age
farmstead.

The centre of activity is the Park Centre,
which is built on the path of the old coach road
(A3) and today welcomes new arrivals much as
did the coaching inn that used to stand near
here many years ago. It is a good place to start
from to gather booklets and information on the
Park and to return to for some light refreshment in the café. A colourful exhibition draws
attention to the objectives of the Park and the
species of birds and animals to look out for,
while various slide programmes and lectures are
given in a small theatre.

As the name implies, the Tree Trail iden-
tifies familiar and lesser-known foliage along
the way. Much of the land now within the Park
was bare hillside shadowed only by the inky

needles of yew. Beech was planted in quantity
in the early Twenties and plantations of Norway spruce, western hemlock and red cedar
followed, with whitebeam, oak and silver birch
establishing themselves naturally.

These extensive beeches have been highly
valued by small local industries over the years.
The wood makes excellent charcoal and was
used for smelting iron ore in the furnaces of the
neighbouring Weald. A glassworks was built
nearby in the 17th century, beech piles were
used to support Winchester Cathedral, and the
wood is pliable and suited to the manufacture
of furniture and kitchen utensils.

Three-and-a-half miles long, the Centre
Trail combines woodland and open downland
walking, with the option of completing only
half. The gravel path passes the spot where a
flint knapper may have sat under a yew tree,
breaking flints. These rocks, which can measure over a foot in length and width, were
widely used throughout Hampshire and Sussex
to build and decorate walls, cottages and
churches. They were also a profitable export
(especially to America) as gun flints for flint-
lock rifles and pistols.

Centuries of sheep have nibbled the soft turf
of the downland and it is studded with wild
flowers at all times of the year. Butterflies such
as the Duke of Burgundy fritillary, flit among
the scrub of gorse and thyme – their larvae feed
on the leaves of the tall-necked cowslip in
spring. Another native is the yellow ant which
creates giant hummocks across the downs. It is
said that the snails which infest the grass and
are in turn eaten by sheep, impart a subtle
flavour to mutton.

Butser Trail offers more of a challenge to the
serious walker. It begins gently, following an
ancient trackway, Lime Kiln Lane. There was
probably an outdoor lime kiln here over a
hundred years ago, where chalk was burnt to
produce building material or fertiliser. At the
foothills of Butser hilltop, known as Little
Butser, is the Ancient Farm Research Trust
Project. Because an attempt is being made to
simulate the conditions under which Iron Age
man lived and worked, the farm is kept isolated. A demonstration area near the Park
Centre provides an interesting précis of the
work being undertaken. Livestock of the
period, Dexter cattle and Soay sheep, are being
reared and ancient crops sown. What would
have been daily chores, such as smelting metal,
firing pottery, spinning and weaving, are completed using the limited tools available to our
ancestors. At the centre of the area is the
largest reconstructed Iron Age 'house' to be
found anywhere.

From the blustery top of Butser Hill there is a
stunning view to every compass point. South is
the busy blue Solent, north the Hogsback; to
the east runs the chalk chain of the South
Downs, while behind, the fields roll through
Hampshire and Berkshire to the West Country. Grazing sheep share the view with
sportsmen. Kite flyers and model gliders har-
ness the wind which whistles over Butser
(sometimes it reaches a gale force 10); hang
gliders use the air currents for their one-way
flight and on summer Sundays, grass skiers may

be seen speeding down the steep green slopes.

The Park has other family attractions, too:
orienteering, pony-trekking, forest drives and
picnic spots. Special events and demonstrations of country crafts and farming skills are
held throughout the year and published in a
calendar of events.

At the heart of the South Downs is Singleton, the home of the Weald and Downland
Museum. Here, among wooded meadowland, historic buildings from the Weald and
Downland areas of Kent, Sussex, Surrey and
Hampshire have been rescued and faithfully
reconstructed. Among them, in this far from
conventional museum, are a charcoal burner's
camp, a wheelwright's shop, a mediaeval farmhouse and a 15th-century granary.

Singleton also has a vineyard which produces Childsdown wine, and there is another
at Hambledon. At both, admission covers a

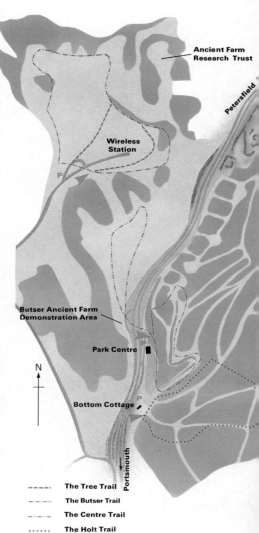

Ancient Farm
Research Trust

Petersfield

Wireless
Station

Butser Ancient Farm
Demonstration Area

Park Centre

N

Bottom Cottage

Portsmouth

- - - - -   The Tree Trail
- · - · -   The Butser Trail
- · · - · ·   The Centre Trail
· · · · · ·   The Holt Trail

tour and a sample tasting. Goodwood House is one of the finest examples of Sussex flintwork, and its rooms are graced with collections of tapestries, porcelain and French and English furniture. Meetings at the famous racecourse culminate in the celebrated event at the end of July – Glorious Goodwood.

Holiday spots along the Sussex coast vary from the organised resort of Bognor Regis to the quiet, unspoilt beaches of the Witterings. There is little choice of campsites in the area, but fishermen fare better, with both river and sea angling. One of the chalk streams visible from Butser Hill is the Meon, and it and its tributary, the East Meon, offer sea and brown trout, while the Western Rother, which flows to join the Arun, has the added promise of barbel. For saltwater sport, the best place to hire a boat is Littlehampton.

Queen Elizabeth Country Park makes a good starting point for walking the eighty-mile long-distance South Downs Way. From here to Beachy Head the path is edged with a profusion of wild flowers, birds and butterflies with picnic sites at Harting Hill and Bo-peep Bostal. Outstanding sights along the route are the Long Man of Wilmington – the figure of a man of uncertain date cut into the chalk and visible for miles; Chanctonbury Ring and Ditchling Beacon. The South Downs Way is also popular with pony trekkers and cyclists.

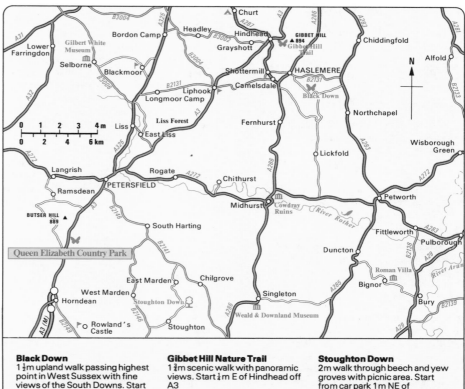

Black Down
1½m upland walk passing highest point in West Sussex with fine views of the South Downs. Start from Black Down car park, 2m S of Haslemere off A286
Open all year

Gibbet Hill Nature Trail
1¾m scenic walk with panoramic views. Start ¼m E of Hindhead off A3
Open all year

Stoughton Down
2m walk through beech and yew groves with picnic area. Start from car park 1m NE of Stoughton (9m S of Petersfield) off B2146
Open all year

Angling
Heath Lake: coarse fishing reservoir at Petersfield
Free fishing for SWA licence holders – see Western Rother
Western Rother: mainly coarse fishing with occasional trout
Daily tickets: Rice Bros, 6 West Street, Midhurst
Tel: (073 081) 3395
Water Authority: SWA, Guildbourne House, Chatsworth Road, Worthing
Tel: (0903) 205252

Camping
Churt: Symondstone farm ▶
Secluded 70-pitch site 5m NW of Haslemere off A287
Open Apr–Oct, must book public holidays

Golfing
Blackmoor:
Tel: (042 03) 2775
Good moorland course 8m N of Petersfield off A325, 18 holes, 6202yds, par 69, SSS70
Liphook:
Tel: (0428) 723271
Easily walked heathland course, 18 holes, 6306yds, par 71, SSS70
Petersfield:
Tel: (0730) 3725
Scenic heathland course recently extended, 18 holes, 5748yds, par 71, SSS68
Rowlands Castle:
Tel: (070 541) 2216
Testing, well-bunkered course 9m S of Petersfield off B2149, 18 holes, 6675yds, par 72, SSS72

General
Bishop's Waltham: Bishop's Waltham Palace: 12th-century residence with 4-storeyed tower
Open all year (ex Mon & Sat)
Hambledon: Vineyard & Winepress: tour plus wine-tasting, 9m SW of Petersfield off B2150
Open Aug–Oct (Sun only 2.30–5.30), plus parties
Tel: (070 132) 475
Midhurst: Cowdray Ruins: remains of 16th-century mansion including notable gatehouse
Open all year daily 10–dusk
Tel: (073 081) 2215
Petersfield: Court House: 14th-century ecclesiastical hall 5m W of Petersfield off A272
Open by appointment only
Tel: (073 087) 274
Selborne: Gilbert White Museum: relics & items of the famous local naturalist
Open Mar–Oct
Tel: (042 050) 275
South Harting: Uppark: late 17th-century mansion with original décor
Open Apr–Sep, Wed, Thu & Sun 2–6

Rolling hills near Selborne

Harlow Trail

Harlow Development
Corporation, Gate House, The
High, Harlow, Essex, CM20 1LJ
Tel: Harlow (0279) 22001

Trail through Harlow's urban fringe
starting at Harlow Museum, off Third
Avenue

Map reference: TL443091

Full 6½-mile trail (short route 2⅔-mile)
showing conservation in an urban
environment with parkland, woods and
farmland

Facilities: unusual ring-bound card file
trail notes with illustrations; car parks in
town centre and at museum

It is easy to associate nature trails with leafy
rambles well off the beaten track and engulfed
in miles of rolling countryside. But to promote
an appreciation of nature and the environment
in Britain's largest new town is a brave and
commendable step. Harlow's Development
Corporation have taken it, with a six-and-a-
half mile, three to four-hour trek around the
fringes of development, where the past rubs
shoulders with the present. A shorter route of
two-and-a-half miles takes only about one-
and-a-half hours; or there is the option of
walking a section at a time.

Harlow has long earned a good reputation
for harmonising the old with the new. When it
was developed, just after the Second World
War, the idea was to incorporate Old Harlow
and three villages in the immediate area. The
biggest sacrifice was borne by agriculture.
Twenty-five farms, some small, others extensive, were affected to make way for the homes
and amenities of an estimated 80 000 people.

Much was kept intact: the old part of town is
still lined with thatched cottages and the scent
of lime tree flowers around St Andrew's church
pervades the air each summer. Even the new
part is given an air of the wide open spaces.
Green lawns intersperse the bricks and mortar
and, rather wistfully, the town's public houses
are named after species of butterfly (Purple
Emperor, Small Copper, White Admiral,
Essex Skipper).

The trail, which keeps one foot in the town
and the other in the country, starts just outside
the centre at the Museum. Cars can be left
either at the town centre or museum car parks,
but even without following this trail, four
wheels are superfluous. Harlow is criss-crossed
by pedestrian byways.

Early steps are uphill and follow the steep
slopes of Willowfield Ravine. There used to be
a stream here, fed from the fields after rainfall,
but since houses, not cereals, now cover the
land, the water rushes into land drains and the
stream only flows occasionally in winter.
Gone, too, are the elm trees that used to stand,
like mighty sentinels, along the path, Dutch
Elm disease claimed them and limes were
planted in their stead.

After crossing Tendring Road, the trail
plunges into a patchwork of homes, gardens,
schools and recreational areas. Harlow is espe-

cially proud of the Bishopfield development.
Flats, maisonettes and patio bungalows
smother a hillside in ordered profusion, each
with a secluded patch of garden. Although too
small for growing much apart from flowers and
rose bushes, the town council has allocated
seventy acres to allotments dotted about between developments. Here the scarlet blooms
of runner beans climb skywards at almost the
same density as the houses at Longbanks (nearly twenty-four to an acre), which lie to the
right of the trail.

Each housing estate has a character of its
own. Barley Croft (the name was taken from a
Tithe map of the 1840s) was built of pre-cast
sections of timber and steel. While Peters-
wood's flats and town houses are of black brick.

Maunds Wood with its oak and coppiced
hornbeam has been here for years, but it is
hardly peaceful. Children have tunnelled into
bramble hedges to make dens and the well-
trodden ground is often scattered with broken
boughs and sweet wrappers. Squirrels are the
only creatures to have withstood the invasion,
but by contrast, Parndon Wood is a quiet
haven where animal and plant life flourish
undisturbed. Nobody is allowed into the Reserve without making an appointment with the
warden.

Much of the trail crosses rolling terrain so
typical of this part of Essex. Fertile boulder clay
and a temperate climate combine to make
excellent arable and dairy farming country.
One of the largest farms is Dorrington, with
300 acres sown with wheat, barley and clover.
Lesser crops are beans and potatoes, but a herd
of Friesian bullocks being raised indoors for
beef, never see the sun.

There is evidence of Saxon and earlier connections around the southern limit of the trail
where the ancient Forest Way is joined. This
long-distance footpath links the forests of Epping and Hatfield, while other tracks lead off
across the countryside to the right and left of
Rye Hill Road. Underfoot the cropped grass is
studded with fleshy plantains and yellow cinquefoil, and hedgerows centuries-old grow
species that would defeat a botanist.

Saxon words can be traced, too. Tye Green
Village, around which much of the new town
has grown, takes its name from *teay* – a clearing
in the forest. Berecroft housing area is derived
from the Anglo-Saxon word for barley – *bere*.
Even Harlow new town has called its municipal
offices Moot Hall.

The villagers of Netteswell would have relied upon the waters of the River Stort to
irrigate their farmland and to drive their mill
wheels, but these days it is used mainly by
coarse fishermen and visitors are welcome.
Further upstream at Stansted Mountfitchet an
18th-century red brick windmill has been restored with much of its machinery and furnishings intact. Scouts now use it as one of their
headquarters.

At Broxbourne on the River Lee, a boat
centre is open in summer months where rowing
and motor boats can be hired by the hour and a
large waterbus carries trippers downstream towards the ruins of Waltham Abbey. Part of the
abbey, the Crypt, is now a museum of local

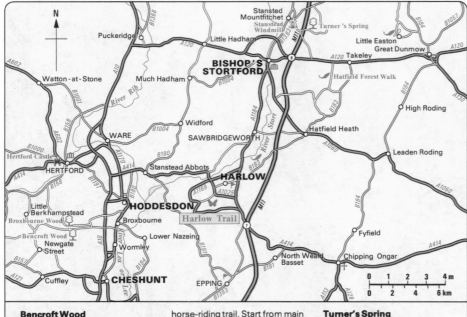

Bencroft Wood
Several signposted 1½–2m trails
through oak and hornbeam
woodland with central pond. Start
from car park White Stubbs Lane,
2m W of Wormley off A10
Open all year

Broxbourne Wood
2m circular walk through 82-acre
conifer wood with picnic area and

horse-riding trail. Start from main
entrance 2m W of Broxbourne
(4m S of Hertford)
Open all year

Hatfield Forest Walk
2m circular trail by marshland
with rich flora and lake. Start from
Takeley Street, 4m E of Bishop's
Stortford off A120
Open all year

Turner's Spring
1½m trail through 6½-acre
woodland reserve. Start from
Stansted Hall, 1½m E of Stansted
Mountfitchet (4m NE of Bishop's
Stortford)
Open all year
Tel: (0279) 53475 (warden)

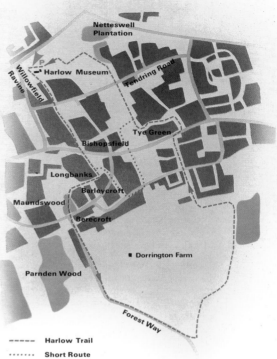

----- **Harlow Trail**

······· **Short Route**

Angling
Little Easton Manor: coarse fishing within stately home grounds near Dunmow
Daily tickets (from riparian owner): Little Easton Manor, Dunmow
Tel: (0371) 2857
Water Authority: AWA, Diploma House, Grammar School Walk, Huntingdon, Cambridgeshire
Tel: (0480) 56181
River Stort: coarse fishing with fair access
Daily tickets: on bank at Burnt Mill Lock, Harlow
Water Authority: TWA, 2nd Floor, Reading Bridge House, Reading
Tel: (0734) 593333

Camping
Chigwell: Grange Farm Leisure Centre ▶▶▶▶
Rural 600-pitch site (300 tents)
Open May–Aug, no bookings

Golfing
Bentley:
Tel: (0277) 73179
Parkland course 2m NW of Brentwood off A128, 18 holes, 6550yds, par 72, SSS72
Epping: Theydon Bois:
Tel: (037 881) 3054
Well-planned open course, 18 holes, 5506yds, par 68, SSS67
Harlow: Canon's Brook:
Tel: (0279) 21482
Easily walked

parkland course, 18 holes, 6801yds, par 73, SSS73

General
Bishop's Stortford: Rhodes Memorial Museum & Commonwealth Centre: many exhibits & items of Cecil Rhodes
Open all year daily 10–4 (ex Sun)
Tel: (0279) 51746
Windmill: restored red brick mill 3m NE of Bishop's Stortford off A11
Open Apr–Oct first Sun in month 2.30–7, plus every Sun in Aug. Other times by appointment
Tel: (0279) 813159
Broxbourne: Broxbourne Zoo: ever-growing animal collection 5m SE of Hertford
Open all year daily 10–6 (5 in winter)
Tel: (099 24) 62852
Chipping Ongar: St Andrews: only extant wooden Saxon church. Accessible at all times
Hertford: Hertford Castle: restored 16th-century gatehouse plus remains of Norman castle
Open all year
Tel: (0992) 54977
Hertford Museum: local history, geology & archaeology
Open all year (ex Sun)
Tel: (0992) 52686
Waltham Abbey: Waltham Abbey, Bridge & Cloisters: 14th-century gatehouse containing crypt museum
Open all year

antiquities. The village whipping post, stocks, pillory and stake (which was said to stop the restless spirit from moving a buried corpse about) are grim reminders of the past. Broxbourne also has a zoo with around 250 species of animals and birds.

At Bishop's Stortford, an 18th-century house is devoted to the memorabilia of Cecil Rhodes and aspects of his life and work in Africa. Hertford Museum has objects of local archaeological and natural history interest – two indoor excursions for dull days.

Hayes Hill Farm, at Waltham Abbey, is a working dairy stand arable farm that specialises in showing city children just how their food is produced. Even those familiar with the country will enjoy the summer demonstrations of country crafts such as wood-turning, corn-dolly making, thatching and sheep shearing.

In the extensive grounds of the Jacobean mansion at Hatfield stands the ancient oak tree in whose shade Elizabeth Tudor was sitting when she heard the news of her succession. It is so old and damaged now that the trunk is propped up on crutches. It symbolises what new towns such as Harlow are doing.

In a changing, shifting world, our national heritage should never be rooted up and discarded; the old and the new can live side by side. That is what makes Harlow Trail unique.

Felbrigg Hall Trails

The National Trust, Blickling, Norwich, NR11 6NF
Tel: Aylsham (026 373) 3471

Off B1436 half way between junction with A148 and Felbrigg village – about 2½ miles south west of Cromer

Map reference: TG194394

Two 1½-mile trails exploring wood and parkland around 17th-century mansion owned by National Trust
Open April–mid-October (*not* Mondays or Fridays)

Facilities: Illustrated trail guides; car park; tea room; picnic place; garden produce shop; mansion with fine library, 18th-century furnishings and paintings

One of the greatest influences on the countryside of the 17th and 18th centuries which has left an indelible impression on today's rural environment, was the estate management practices of the landed gentry. They preserved the shape of woodlands with their park walls, brought some rationale to commercial forestry, planted new functional and ornamental woodlands and furthered field division. This was also the birth of the era of the fashionable landscape gardener, a breed who, with their employers, could hardly afford to ignore the fact that, however picturesque their efforts became, parks were very much a part of profitable working estates.

These influences were brought to play in the development of Felbrigg Hall, a mid-17th- and early 18th-century manor donated to the National Trust in 1969 by Robert Wyndham Ketton-Cremer. Just how permanent they have remained can be seen along the two trails laid out through the park and woodland of the hall grounds – the beautiful Lakeside and Woodland Walks.

Felbrigg Hall was partly built and the park developed by William Windham I and his grandson William Windham II. The plans for the West Wing are dated at 1675 and a fine ceiling in the drawing room at 1687. The Jacobean south part of the house predates this by some fifty years. It has a tall parapet and over the three protruding bays are carved the words *Gloria Deo in excelsis*. The Woodland Walk explores the former deer park and old beech forest north of the hall and the Lakeside Walk looks at some of the farmland and the ornamental lake to the south – both are approximately one-and-a-half miles long. All the hall grounds are being carefully managed to preserve the wildlife and keeping to the paths is a necessary part of this.

Early parts of the woodland walk are called the Primrose Walk (the flowers will be obvious in spring) and take you through the deer park now quite well wooded with sycamore and beech. Some of the sweet chestnuts you see may be up to 300 years old and are probably survivors from the tree cultivating nursery set up by William Windham I to provide both ornamental trees and to restock his forests. Before entering the Great Wood, the path makes a tour through a small stretch of heathland where the sandy subsoil will support only a rough undergrowth of bracken and brambles and where the dominant trees are pine and silver birch. The heathland leads uphill to the regimented plantation of conifers, part of the woodland the National Trust has invested in, with Forestry Commission help.

Throughout the walk you may have seen uncleared wood debris, dead trunks and other superb habitats for birds, mammals and insects. Less obvious is the fact that much bramble undergrowth has also been encouraged to develop and provide nesting sites. Birds of the Felbrigg woods and gardens include the great spotted woodpecker, the redstart, the

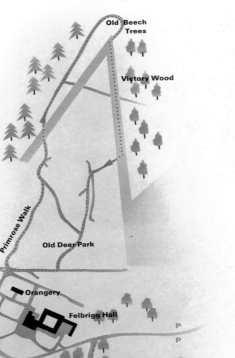

The Great Wood

Old Beech Trees

Victory Wood

Primrose Walk

Old Deer Park

Orangery

Felbrigg Hall

P
P

St. Margaret's Church

The Woodland Walk ·······
The Lakeside Walk - - - -

Jubilee Clump

Felbrigg Hall

nuthatch and the tiny wren. The conifers harbour the red squirrel, its population sadly diminishing in the continuing onslaught from its hardier (and less attractive) grey cousin. Rarely seen, but here in numbers, is the stoat.

Emerging from the conifers, the path enters the Great Wood, a dense remnant of what was, for thousands of years a natural beech forest. Some of the trees are over 300 years old and top 100 feet – many are pollarded above the reach of feeding cattle and deer. Fencing stakes and firewood would be cut regularly from the new growths on the trunk. Part of the Great Wood is known as Victory Wood – it was planted at the end of the Second World War with conifers. The return to the house is along a ride which has been mowed and cleared to a pattern which gives three types of plant and animal habitat. This ride brings you back into the deer park trees and a quarter-mile stroll to reach the end of the trail.

While the Lakeside Walk is named for its track around the Hall's lake, formed from a series of stocked fish pools in the mid-18th century, it ranges far wider than that. It sets out from close to the Hall's Orangery greenhouse through a woodland, its fringe dotted with wild cherry trees, which give way to the more mature of the old Park trees – oak and sweet chestnut. The lake, a common feature of landscaping in 18th century, was not all that the second William Windham's plans involved. Woodland, hedges, walls and outbuildings were razed to open the view between the house and the lake – to little avail as the water can barely be seen below the Park's rise, over the slope of Roundwood Hill.

A haunt of moorhen, coot and duck, the lake has considerable stocks of coarse fish such as eel, tench, perch and pike which can be fished on day tickets available from the Hall. Herons may be seen fishing the periphery – the bigger birds here are Canada goose and the mute swan. Past the lake, in a high corner of the Park grounds, is a small clump of oak and beech planted to celebrate Queen Elizabeth's Jubilee.

St Margaret's church, a favourite of Sir John Betjeman's, containing monuments by Nollekens and Grinling Gibbons, marks the path's western limit. At one time, Felbrigg village will certainly have been scattered around the church – it is not identified at what time the Plague forced a move to its present location over half a mile away.

While you are at Felbrigg, do not fail to visit the walled garden – produce from it is on sale at the Hall during the summer. After your glimpse of the Hall's delights, you can take tea, browse through the library or eat in the garden area set aside for picnics.

Felbrigg is only two miles from the coast resort of Cromer, its sandy beach fringed by lofty cliffs. Famed for crabs (and with a bit of luck you may get lobster here, too) the fishing boats work from the beach alongside the pier and lifeboat house. Amusements centre around the pier but the town also has a lifeboat museum at the foot of The Gangway, a five-acre zoo (lions, leopards, bears and monkeys) and a museum in a row of small fishermen's cottages. Sea anglers along this coast can expect catches of bass, cod, dab, flounder and plaice.

Very active local conservationists have made Norfolk a county of Nature Reserves but no visit to the northern part of the county would be complete without a visit to the Broads Reserve of Hickling. Formed by peat digging and land drainage schemes, the Broads are a fascinating haven of wildlife. Members of the Norfolk Naturalists' Trust give commentaries on boat trips of Hickling Broad, Horsey Mere and Martham Broad Reserves, or you can visit a selection of observation hides by arrangement with the Trust. Boats leave from the Pleasure Boat Inn, Hickling.

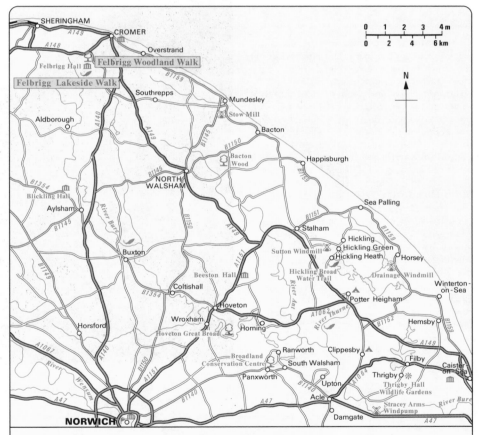

Bacton Wood Forest Trail
1½m woodland walk with numerous plant species. Start at Wensum Forest, 2m E of North Walsham off B1150
Open all year

Broadland Conservation Centre Nature trail
¼m signposted walk through alder wood to open broad. Start from Ranworth Staith, Ranworth off B1140 at Panxworth
Open Apr–Oct

Hickling Broad Water Trail
2½m conducted tour by boat and on foot including bird hides, sedge beds and observation tower. Start at The Pleasure Boat Inn, Hickling off A149 at Stalham
Open Jun–Sep, Tue–Thu, must book in advance
Tel: (069 261) 562

Hoveton Great Broad Nature Trail
½m circular walk along narrow woodland path with midway observation hide. Start from north bank of River Bure, 2½m downstream from Wroxham
Open May–mid-Sep

Lion Wood
1m trail through oak and beech trees, rich in birds. Start at park pavilion, Woodrow Pilling Park, Harvey Lane, Norwich
Open all year

Gibraltar Point Nature Reserve

Lincolnshire and South Humberside Trust for Nature Conservation, Gibraltar Point, Skegness, Lincolnshire
(and at Manor House, Alford, Lincolnshire)
Tel: Skegness (0754) 2677

At end of Gibraltar Road, 3 miles south of Skegness town centre

Map reference: TF555581

1-mile long Reserve with marked paths which can be followed at will – principal features are the duneland and saltmarsh environments

Facilities: Very informative illustrated brochure; visitors' centre with exhibitions of Reserve research; 3 car parks; beach

Burgh-le-Marsh windmill

Of all the many natural changes that are taking place in the environment, those that occur at the fringe between sea and land are often the most dramatic. The constant erosion and deposition of mud and sand by tide, currents, waves and wind, often accelerated by man, present a changing coastline which can show a tremendous number of differing habitats within a very small area. Such a place is Gibraltar Point, three miles south of the Lincolnshire resort of Skegness, a 1500-acre Nature Reserve designed and managed by the Lincolnshire and South Humberside Trust on behalf of Nature Conservation.

Gibraltar Point not only marks a dramatic change-point of the east coast – a sandy promontory between the dune banks that stretch down from the Humber and the salt marshes of the Wash – it is itself in the process of extending out into the sea. Sited to the east of an extensive area of former marshland which has been steadily won from the sea since mediaeval times, the Point once extended slightly further south. Now, spits of sand are developing parallel to the Point's east shore. These will eventually produce colonisation by plants enabling the sand to rise above the water level permanently and become new duneland.

Between this area of dune development and the mouth of the Steeping River, extensively canalised for drainage in its flow across the Steeping and Wainfleet lowlands, paths have been laid out which are marked by numbered posts. It is the Lincolnshire Trusts's policy simply to provide visitors with a full and informative booklet on the Reserve and then allow them to use the paths at will to explore the many interesting facets of the Point's marshland, fresh and brackish pools and sand habitats. The Reserve's field station, a building developed by extending a former Coastguard lookout point, and Visitors' Centre are at the

end of the West Dunes, which were the site of the actual coast about 200 or so years ago.

The land between the West and East Dunes is a marsh, much of which is flooded up to the earthwork rampart of Bulldog Bank. Behind the bank, recently heightened to prevent sea flooding, is a freshwater marsh. Most of the dry dune areas are covered with the spiky bushes of sea buckthorn, its drab grey-green foliage alleviated in autumn and early winter by the vivid orange of its berries. On older-established dunes, it is possible to see that the buckthorn gives way to other shrubs such as privet (the wild species), elder and hawthorn. Towards the sea, the dunes are bound and

protected against wind erosion by marram grass. The tall clumps themselves collect sand and add to the dunes' stature. Behind this area of generation there is a completely different flora of shorter plants such as sea fescue grass, chickweed and the yellow-flowered ragwort.

In the developing area of the shoreline, Gibraltar Point shows all the stages of dune growth. As the dunes rise above the high water mark by deposition, the tide line becomes marked by the arrival of wrack – plant debris, skate egg cases and those curiosities, the sea firs (actually congregations of small organisms related to coral). This material helps bind more sand and becomes a mulch in which salt-adapted plants such as the saltwort and sea rocket can begin to colonise the new sand. Where the water flow deposits mud, the fleshy (and edible) tufts of samphire can be seen and cord grass (*Spartina maritima*) begins to bind the silt.

The strip saltings with their sub-culture of snails and small molluscs are a great attraction to flocks of birds. Little terns and ringed plovers are among the regular nesting colonies on the sand of the Spit (a developing dune) habitat. Waders inhabit the shallows of the marshes in their autumn passage to warmer climates or for a winter's stay. Among regular residents and visitors are dunlins, herring and black-headed gulls and oyster-catchers.

Within the Reserve are two further favourites with the birds – the Mill Pool and the Mere. The Mill Pool is an extremely deep, artificial pond holding fresh water which seeps from the very high water table. In the rush fringes, moorhens and sedge-warblers nest. Also man-made, the Mere is a purpose-built bird observation lake of fairly shallow fresh water. Public access is restricted to the hide at its western corner. Attracted to the Mere are herons, teals, grebes, dunlins and shelducks (the last a winter visitor), among dozens of other species. Frogs and toads inhabit the fringes and the Trust reports sightings of grass snakes swimming here.

The Point's mammal life is not quite so prominently on display. In the areas of heavy shrub cover, the Reserve supports a considerable population of small rodents such as the pigmy and common shrews and the short-tailed vole. Keeping them in check is a trio of birds of prey, the short-eared owl, the kestrel and, on occasion, the rare harrier. While foxes do not, at the moment, inhabit the Reserve, there is a considerable population of them locally and it has been necessary to wire off the nesting area of the Spit to prevent them from getting at sitting birds, eggs and young.

For a panorama across the whole Reserve and the flat surrounding countryside of reclaimed marshes, you can ascend to the top of Mill Hill, which is probably the oldest dune in the area and is certainly the tallest. There is a view to the chalk uplands of the Wolds where the Steeping River rises as the Lymn (thought by many to be Tennyson's *Brook*) and in the opposite direction, the strip saltings which are the indication that this area will continue to develop and change.

To the north of the Reserve is the bustling resort of Skegness, well-known for its bracing airs, for which Tennyson was an enthusiast. The town's unusual name is probably derived from the name of one of the 8th-century Danish invaders of Britain, the chieftain, Skeggi. From a fishing port, the resort has now developed into a spacious town of wide avenues, tree-lined streets and extensive sea-front gardens. For the family it has all the fun of the fair and a wide choice of accommodation from a holiday camp to the campsite in Richmond Drive.

Skegness is still a fishing centre for the leisure angler, with local charter and hire boats fishing the banks off the town and Gibraltar

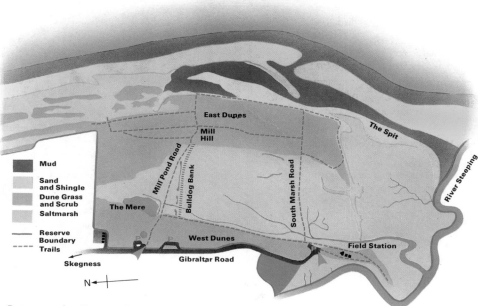

Point or the Boston Deeps to the south. Catches include cod, dogfish, mackerel, ray, tope and whiting. Fishing for bream and roach on the Steeping River is controlled by the Anglian Water Authority and the Witham and District Anglers' Federation. Skegness's Golf Club, its links laid out on the dunes between the town and Gibraltar Point, welcomes holiday and touring visitors.

Five miles inland is the tiny town of Burgh-le-Marsh, with its fully restored mid-19th-century windmill. Visitors can see four floors of the mill, which is a five-sailed design in working order.

If you take the back roads on your return to Skegness, you will find the Church Farm Museum, a fascinating living museum of 19th-century fenland farming, including a historic collection of farm implements, and workshops where visitors can buy from a selection of examples of rural crafts.

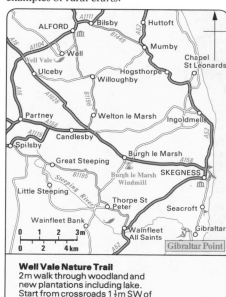

Well Vale Nature Trail
2m walk through woodland and new plantations including lake. Start from crossroads 1½m SW of Alford on A1104
Open Jul–Aug, Tue, Fri & Sat 11–5

Angling
Bell Water Drain: small coarse fishery near Thorpe Culvert
Daily tickets: Boston Angling Association (J D Maguire), 6 Churchill Drive, Boston
Tel: (0205) 64949
Water Authority: as River Steeping
River Steeping: coarse fishing for mainly roach
Daily tickets: Witham & District Joint Anglers' Federation (R Hobley), 30 Gunby Avenue, Lincoln
Tel: (0522) 683688
Water Authority: AWA (Lincs Rivers Division), Diploma House, Grammar School Walk, Huntingdon
Tel: (0480) 56181

Camping
Skegness: Richmond Drive Carapark ►►►
Tel: (0754) 2097
Level 100-pitch site (no tents)
Open Apr–mid-Sep, must book Jul–Aug

Golfing
Sandilands:
Tel: (0521) 41432
Flattish links course 1½m S of Sutton-on-Sea off A52, 18 holes, 5984yds, par 70, SSS69
Skegness: North Shore:
Tel: (0754) 3298
Easily walked parkland course, 18 holes, 6010yds, par 71, SSS69
Seacroft:
Tel: (0754) 3020
Flat seaside course,

18 holes, 6478yds, par 71, SSS71

Riding
Coningsby: Ivy Lane Riding School & Livery Stables (J Phillips), Ivy Lane, Coningsby
Tel: (0526) 42461

General
Alford: Alford Manor House: museum with varied exhibits housed in 16th-century building
Open Tue & Fri for further information
Tel: (052 12) 6247
Mawthorpe Collection of Bygones: fascinating display of farm & domestic crafts & implements
Open all year
Tel: (052 12) 2336
Boston: Fydell House: 18th-century Georgian mansion
Open Mon–Fri 10–6 during term time
Tel: (0205) 63116
Skegness: Burgh-le-Marsh Windmill: 19th-century 5-sailed tower windmill in working order, 5m W of Skegness off A158
Tel: (0754) 810281
Church farm museum: collection depicting 19th-century rural life
Open Apr–Oct daily 10.30–5.30
Tel: (0754) 66658
Skegness Natureland Marine Zoo: modern marine zoo & sanctuary
Open all year daily 10–7.30 (10–4 in winter)
Tel: (0754) 4345

Clumber Park Nature Walks

The National Trust, Clumber Park, Worksop, Nottinghamshire, S80 3BE

Tel: Worksop (0909) 86411

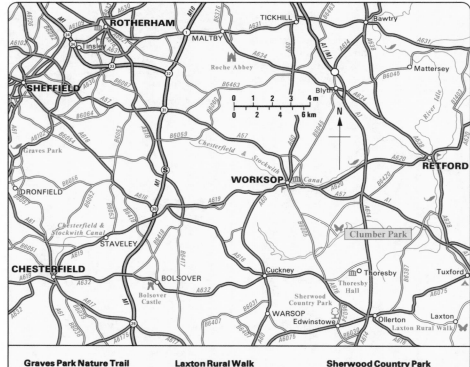

3 miles south east of Worksop off B6005 – signposted Carburton and Clumber Park

Map reference: SK626747

Two walks of 3 miles and 1 mile showing conservation and restoration of a Capability Brown landscape in a former ducal hunting park – park open all year (some facilities closed Fridays and weekdays from November to March)

Facilities: Illustrated trail brochure; car parks; picnic places; tea shop; information centre; fishing

Two nature walks encompass most of the features north and south of the former home of the Dukes of Newcastle in this park.

Walking the Heart of the Park, you start at the Trust's information centre, close to the site of the old house. The walk passes the Paddocks where the Duke's horses were cloistered for foaling and the hall's enormous kitchen gardens before entering Ash Tree Hill wood. This particular wood is some seventy acres of Scots pine, larch, sycamore and ash, parts of which were replanted in 1934. Remember that all

these woods are on ground that was once bracken and heather heath, perhaps dotted with trees in very small clumps. The rhododendrons you see were introduced both for ornament and as a habitat in which game birds could shelter.

The path drops down from the middle of the wood (Junction Hill) to the ornamental one-and-a-quarter-mile lake created by damming the River Poulter. This is the same stream which also forms the four-mile Great Lake of Welbeck. The island you see was created to prevent vandals from harming nesting swans. Another amusing water resident here is the diving bird, the great crested grebe, keeping company with a considerable population of mallard, coot and moorhen. The tufted duck differs from the mallard as, like the grebe it is a diver – the mallard up-ends itself in the water, searching weed stems and bottom for its food. You may fish in the lake. Day tickets are issued to angle for the lake's stock of coarse fish which include pike, bream, and roach.

The last half of this walk is through the White Pheasant and Osberton Round Woods to the feature for which Clumber is world-famous. It is an avenue of lime trees two miles long, twin ranks of the common variety marching through Hardwick Wood to the present A614. Not the work of Brown, who would have scorned its intrusion on his brand of natural landscape, the avenue was planted some 155 years ago. There are nearly 1300 trees which, like all limes, constantly regenerate small shoots from the trunk base. These are cut regularly and the ravages of moth caterpillars feeding on the leaves are checked by grease bands on the trunk to trap adult egg layers.

Clumber's South Lawns walk is a trip around the poor pasture of the parkland on the opposite bank of the lake from the former hall. Starting by a young pine plantation, called the Edwinstowe Round, the path goes down to the lake shore through bracken and scattered oaks to the rough *Molinia* grass of the Lawns – an addition of a mile or so to the main walk which enables you to see more of the lake.

Graves Park Nature Trail
1½m woodland walk alongside stream. Start 3m S of Sheffield off A61 after B6068 junction
Open all year

Laxton Rural Walk
6m circular trail across fields and through villages. Start at Laxton village, 3m SW of Tuxford off A611
Open all year

Sherwood Country Park
1m wood and heathland trail with Robin Hood associations. Start at Sherwood Forest visitor centre, Edwinstowe, 10m S of Worksop off B6034
Open all year

Wales & West Midlands

3

Christchurch Forest Trail

The Forestry Commission, Crown Offices, Coleford, Forest of Dean, Gloucestershire

Off B4228 ¾ mile north of junction with A4136 at Lower Berry Hill – signposted to campsites

Map reference: SO568129

2½-mile trail through ancient and modern afforestation of deciduous and coniferous trees – passes mine-workings, charcoal hearth and woodpecker haunts

Facilities: Illustrated trail brochure; car park; campsites; well-stocked food shop; picnic sites – eleven other nearby trails

One of the delights of being a camper or caravanner is that a long-distance footpath, a nature trail or a bridleway may be right on the doorstep of the campsite. Such is the case in the Forest of Dean, where every family on holiday at Bracelands or Christchurch site may follow at least one of the twelve forest trails.

Boxed in by the River Wye, the Welsh border and the Severn estuary, the Forest of Dean is one of the few Royal hunting forests of England to have survived the onslaught of man, his buildings and machines. It was far from being only a playground for the rich. The inhabitants were hard-working miners, shepherds and charcoal burners.

A pre-historic forest which once covered the land, fossilised into coal measures. Small mines were opened and worked for more than 500 years. They still are today, under a privilege of Free Mining granted by Edward I. Iron ore was taken from Clearwell Caves until as recently as 1945, a process which had gone on for 3000 years when the Romans were laying their roads through the Forest. Stretches of these straight routes still remain at Blakeney.

Charcoal was needed to smelt the ore and so produce iron, and at one time, every clearing in the woods would have supported a lonely charcoal burner and his beehive-like hearth. With careful searching, it is possible to locate former sites.

Another craftsman of the Forest is the stone cutter. Pennant Blue Sandstone is quarried at Bixhead, and Forest Marble, as the cut stone is called, has gone into the construction of many fine buildings, among them the Severn and Tamar bridges. Sadly, this industry has declined also, and the Forest of Dean is left with two major money earners – forestry and tourism.

The two are compatible, thanks to the Forestry Commission's tight rein on 700 000 visitors to the area. Every information booklet and notice reminds them of the dangers of fire and their responsibilities to the countryside.

Christchurch Forest trail starts at Christchurch campsite and ventures two-and-a-half-miles into High Meadow Woods. Many of the trees here are among the oldest in the Forest – oaks over 200 years old – while others, such as the western hemlock, were planted fairly recently. The most cost-effective trees are fast-growing softwoods – Norway spruce with its white timber is in demand for papermaking; and European, Japanese and hybrid larches for boat building and fencing. Although oaks are no longer used for ships' timbers, the trees are still planted, along with beech, to preserve the character of the Forest.

The oak is also important for the conservation of wildlife. Each tree supports an incredible 324 species of insects, apart from mosses and lichens and a vast bird population which lives, in turn, on the insects. Its only enemy is the grey squirrel which, in summer, devastates the bark, inflicting fatal damage to many young oaks and other broadleaves. Only slightly less damage is done by fallow deer bucks in autumn, when they rub their new antlers against immature trees and so fray the bark. In both cases, the numbers of squirrels and deer is controlled so that the damage does not get out of hand.

A harmless inhabitant of the Forest is the badger, and the trail passes a disused sett which acts like a show house, with the earth and old

Angling

Hartpury Lake: good mixed fishing 5m NW of Gloucester
Daily tickets (in advance):
Watersmeet Motel, Hartpury
Tel: (045 270) 358
No licence required
River Wye: renowned for salmon
Daily tickets: Royal Hotel, Symonds Yat
Tel: (0600) 890238
Water Authority: WNWDA, Cambrian Way, Brecon
Tel: (0874) 3181

Camping

Christchurch: Bracelands/ Christchurch: two full facilities sites.
Booking at main reception office, off B4228 at Berry Hill
Tel: (059 43) 3376
Open mid-Mar–Oct
Worcester Lodge/ Woodland: two minimal facilities sites in wooded clearings
Bookings & opening dates as Bracelands/ Christchurch
Mitchel Troy: Glen Trothy Caravan & Camping Site ▶▶
Tel: (0600) 2295
Level 76-pitch site near river
Open Apr–Oct, must book public holidays

Golfing

Lydney:
Tel: (059 44) 2614
Flat parkland course with windy fairways, 9 holes, 5780yds, par 68, SSS68
Ross-on-Wye (Gorsley):
Tel: (098 982) 267
Rolling parkland course with tight, well-screened fairways, 18 holes, 6491yds, par 72, SSS72

General

Chapel Hill: Tintern Abbey: extensive remains of 13th-century Cistercian church, 5m N of Chepstow off A466
Open all year
Clearwell: Clearwell Castle: mock-Gothic castle with Regency interior, plus bird park
Open Apr–Sep (ex Mon & Sat)
Clearwell Caves & Ancient Iron Mines: local mining & geological site with picnic area
Open Easter–Sep (ex Mon & Sat)
Tel: (0594) 23700
For off-season party booking
Gloucester: Bishop Hooper's Lodging: three 16th-century timber-framed buildings housing craft & industry exhibits
Open all year daily 10–5 (ex Sun)
Tel: (0452) 26467
City Museum & Art Gallery: archaeology, glass & silver collections
Open all year daily 10–5 (ex Sun)
Tel: (0452) 24131
Goodrich: Goodrich Castle: 12th–14th-century fortress
Open all year
Newent: The Birds of Prey Conservation & Falconry Centre: numerous trained birds plus interesting museum, 9m E of Ross-on-Wye
Open Feb–Nov daily 10.30–5.30 (ex Tue)
Tel: (0531) 820286
Lydney: Dean Forest Railway: working branch line from Lydney through forest – for steam days see local press
or
Tel: (045 276) 559
Westbury-on-Severn: Westbury Court garden: unique 17th-century water-garden layout, now within National Trust
Open May–Sep (ex Mon & Tue), plus Apr & Oct weekends only

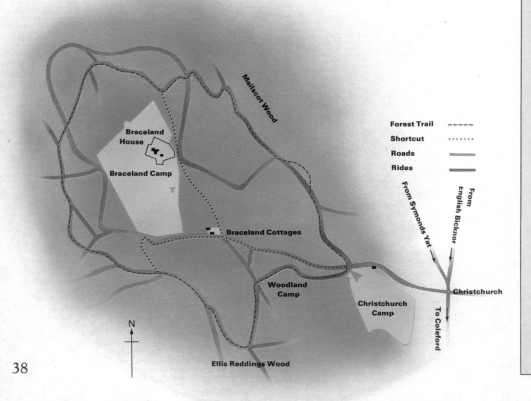

Braceland House
Braceland Camp
Mallscot Wood
Braceland Cottages
Woodland Camp
Christchurch Camp
From Symonds Yat
From English Bicknor
Christchurch
To Coleford
Ellis Reddings Wood

Forest Trail -----
Shortcut ....
Roads ———
Rides ———

N

bedding thrown out in heaps by each doorway. After a night fall of rain, his distinctive footprints can be spotted on a well-worn path: broader than a Labrador's paw with five toes and long toenails.

Where the trail invades coniferous plantations, the forest floor is bare except for hummocks of spruce needles – the nests of the brown wood ant, lichens and fungi. Where there is more light, bracken and bramble are found, and the delicious purple berries of the wortleberry.

Another forest trail of the same length is the curiously-named Boy's Grave and Cannop Forest Trail. Here the emphasis is less on the plantations of the Forestry Commission and more on the natural features of this part of the Forest, and the part man has played. The name probably derives from the Norman French *'bois greve'*, meaning a sloping wood. A more colourful legend tells of the tragic death of a gypsy boy and how he was buried by an ancient oak – which no longer remains.

A stream, rising from a spring at Black Penny Wall Well at the start of the walk, accompanies the trail for much of the way. At one point it is diverted into a small pool where water-loving plants grow – tall alders, rushes, foxgloves and hard-fern. Further on are two man-made lakes, particularly popular with picnickers and fishermen. Broad swaths of grass are kept short by the constant traffic of visitors in summer but around the lakes are masses of ferns and reeds. Cannop Ponds are stocked with coarse fish – tench, bream, perch and chub, and the Forestry Commission leases the fishing rights to Yorkley and District Angling Club. A Severn River Authority licence and a day ticket authorise newcomers.

Nearby are the Forest of Dean Stone Firms which have quarried and cut massive blocks of sandstone into building stones. This sandstone is banded by seams of coal, some too thin to be worked. The freeminers gave names to the sites

they dug, 'Breadless', 'No Coal' and 'Little' were obviously less fruitful than others.

The Wilderness Countryside Trails are arranged in three loops (two of one-and-a-half miles, the other two miles long). Each can be walked separately or together, and trace the history of the Forest and draw attention to the future and the possibility of encroachment by farming.

New Fancy Trail is for the rambler who enjoys a quiet pace along a level footpath. It

takes its name from a colliery which was closed in 1944, and at first follows a disused railway cutting.

By contrast, steam engines are very much alive in another part of the Forest. Norchard Steam Centre holds open days in summer when its mighty engines puff along four miles of track, bringing nostalgia or a new experience to their passengers.

Since the Clearwell Caves stopped mining, only visitors have been inside to see a collection of geological samples and typical mining equipment used throughout the years.

The most popular tourist attraction of the area is the sinuous, slow-running River Wye. Although it has a reputation for its record-breaking catches of salmon, very few stretches are available to the visiting angler, and most just admire it from afar. One of the most stunning views is from the 472-foot Yat Rock, which overlooks the narrow gorge of Symonds Yat. Another vantage point is from the Tudor-timbered town of Ross-on-Wye, although it becomes choked with trippers at summer weekends.

Since the Forest is bordered on one side by the Severn Estuary, the A48 is one of the best places to see the Severn Bore. Although a frequent occurrence, bores of any great size happen on about twenty-five days of the year.

Golfers can pit their wits against the tricky parkland and meadowland championship course of St Pierre, just over the border into Wales at Chepstow. This pleasant border town has a ruined castle overlooking a broad sweep in the Wye and a fascinating museum which catalogues the town's former industries, salmon fishing and the wine trade.

Biblins Adventure Trail
4m woodland walk featuring fallow deer and badgers. Start at footbridge over River Wye, 1m SW of Symonds Yat
Open all year

Boy's Grave & Cannop Forest Trail
2½m walk through mixed woodland with midway picnic area. Start ¾m S of B4226/B4234 crossroads
Open all year

Edge End Forest Trail
3¼m walk through developing forestland. Start 2m NE of Coleford off A4136
Open all year

Speech House Trail
2½m walk through mixed woodland. Start midway between Cinderford and Coleford off B4226
Open all year

Symonds Yat Forest Trail
2m walk through conifer trees depicting geology of Wye gorge. Start at log cabin (refreshment hut) near Symonds Yat Rock off B4432
Open all year

Wenchford Forest Trail
4m walk including relics of ancient forestry life. Start 1½m NW Blakeney
Open all year

River Wye seen from Symonds Yat

Oxwich National Nature Reserve

Nature Conservancy Council,
Oxwich Reserve Centre, Oxwich,
Swansea, SA3 1LS
Tel: (Gower (044 120) 320

1½ miles off the A4118 on unclassified road 11 miles west of Swansea – signposted Oxwich

Map reference: SS502865

Two trails in small coastal National Nature Reserve: Sand Dunes Trail – ¾-mile walk illustrating dune erosion and deposition; Woodland Walk – 3-mile walk through cliffside woodland and pasture

Facilities: illustrated trail brochures; exhibitions in reserve centre; car park; public beach

---

Flanked by the Bristol Channel to the south and west and Carmarthen Bay to the north, the eighteen-mile-long Gower Peninsula has imposing limestone cliffs which are an echo of the Pembrokeshire coast to the west. It has been inhabited since Palaeolithic times, as human remains discovered in the Gower's many caves show, an iron age camp survives at Cil Ifor and the Normans left behind defensive earthworks and fortifications. The variety of the Gower coastline, with cliffs to the south and salt marshes to the north, has led to the establishment of three Nature Reserves at Whitford Burrows, Rhossili (the Gower Coast reserve) and Oxwich. On the Oxwich Reserve, its sandy beach a popular venue for holidaying and weekend tourists, the Nature Conservancy Council has designed two nature trails. They show two facets of the natural history – the habitat of the sand dunes and the contrasting flora and fauna of Oxwich Woods and the coastal farmland.

The Sand Dunes Trail is a three-quarter of a mile loop from the beach car park around a section of the Oxwich Burrows sand dunes. As you set out, notice that the steep woods of Nicholaston to the north east of the Reserve Centre were once the coast; a deep bay has been eroded by the sea from a stretch of softer shaly rocks enclosed by limestone headlands. The sea steadily retreated as land emerged under the twin influences of tides and wind.

The first event in the formation of land was the formation of a vast shingle bank which was then covered to a considerable depth with wind-blown sand. This event took place about 2500 years ago and the dunes have been advancing out into the sea ever since as the sand became stabilised by plants and accrued more wind and wave-transported material. Oxwich's early dunes were stabilised by sea couch grass and other plants able to grow up as more sand was caught by their leaves – sea rocket, prickly saltwort and succulent sandwort are others that create the sand traps. As the dune becomes more established and higher, marram grass with its long underground stems takes over as the main binding agent.

Where this primitive cover is broken by the trampling of beach visitors' feet, or the creation of the car park, the sand becomes as mobile as ever and is blown away inland by the strong prevailing winds. Wind can shift sand by the ton and there are several points on the trail where this erosion can be seen. The Nature Conservancy Council is countering the erosion by fencing off vulnerable areas, planting marram grass and installing brushwood hedges which cut down the wind enough to allow the growth of new embryo dunes.

While yellow sand can still be seen between the plants, the dune is still subject to erosion and deposition, so it is called a 'mobile dune'. However, once established and carpeted with a good layer of humus, other plants begin to appear and the dune is considered fixed and some times called a 'grey dune'. Bracken, mosses and lichens are the most primitive followers on of the marram – but the more long-standing dunes also have dewberry (one of the many *Rubus* blackberry species that are found within the area), wild strawberry and rangy wild privet.

As the walk returns to the centre, it passes marshland trapped behind the dunes. Once the high tides would have flooded the area behind the shingle banks and dunes but during the 18th century, the Penrice Castle estate drained the land and made grazing land. Pools and ponds were landscaped into the reclaimed land but the drainage system fell into disuse and the land is now largely freshwater marsh. Saltmarsh lies outside the sea wall. The marsh is closed to visitors as it is an important bird breeding ground but as you pass by you will see reed and sedge warblers, heron, ducks and grebes.

Oxwich's Woodland Walk runs south from the point where you return from the dunes and starts behind the seaside church which is almost on the beach. The wooded cliff is limestone which was quarried during the 19th-century – the lime was kilned and used for cement and as an alkali with which to neutralise acid soils in agriculture. The dominant species in the wood is sycamore but clearings have been made where oak and ash can grow free from choking by sycamore seedlings.

Lower parts of the wood are very damp and shaded, ideal conditions for wild garlic which grows in profusion. Close up, you should be able to smell its characteristic odour. In the higher parts of the wood, the soil is drier and the wood floor is a carpet of dogs mercury with a scattered undergrowth of privet. At the top of the woods and having passed through a scrub of tall bracken fern and then a former pasture (now a mix of both common and western gorse) you will reach an Ordnance Survey triangulation point which is 280ft above sea level. From here there is a panorama of the Bristol Channel as far as Lundy Island and down the Gower's south coast to Rhossili.

The path continues over rough grass pasture to the clifftop of Oxwich Point, where you will find primrose growing and rock ledges supporting clumps of common rock rose and tormentil, both yellow-flowering. Heather also grows here, despite its normal phobia for lime soils.

Angling
Glyn Clydach Pond: coarse fishing water at Neath
Daily tickets (in advance): Neath & Dulais Angling Club (A Beasley), 12 Briton Ferry Road, Neath
Water Authority: as River Tawe
Port Eynon: good shore fishing for bass at Fall Bay. Large tope at Oxwich Point
River Tawe: fair sea trout following recent recovery from pollution
Daily tickets: Capstan House, Beach Street, Swansea
Tel: (0792) 54756
Water Authority: WNWDA, Cambrian Way, Brecon
Tel: (0874) 3181

Camping
Fairwood: Blackhills Caravan Park ►
Tel: (0792) 27065
Level 300-pitch site 6m W of Swansea off B4271
Open Apr–Oct, must book Jul–Aug

Golfing
Clyne:
Tel: (0792) 66589
Wind-exposed heathland course midway between Swansea & Mumbles, 18 holes, 6267yds, par 70, SSS70
Fairwood Park:
Tel: (0792) 23648
Parkland course W of Swansea near airport, 18 holes, 6704yds, par 72
Pennard:
Tel: (044 128) 3131
Undulating links course 1m W of Bishopston off B4436, 18 holes, 6266yds, SSS71
Swansea Bay:
Tel: (0792) 812198
Flattish seaside course, 18 holes, 6417yds, par 72, SSS71

General
Llanrhidian: Weobley Castle 12th–14th-century fortified manor
Open Apr–Sep, daily 10–7 (Sun 1–7), plus 10–4 in winter (Sun 1–4)
Mumbles: Oystermouth Castle: ruined chapel & gatehouse of 13th/14th-century stronghold
Open all year
Tel: (0792) 50821 ext 2815
Neath: Neath Abbey: ruins of 12th-century Cistercian abbey
Open all year
Penscynor Wildlife Park: bird garden, monkeys & tropical fish
Open all year daily 10–6
Tel: (0639) 2189
Swansea: Glynn Vivian Art Gallery & Museum: contemporary British artists, plus local porcelain & pottery
Open all year weekdays 10.30–5.30
Tel: (0792) 55006
Maritime & Industrial Museum: wool mill production, transport & steam exhibits
Open all year weekdays 10.30–5.30
Tel: (0792) 55006/ 53051

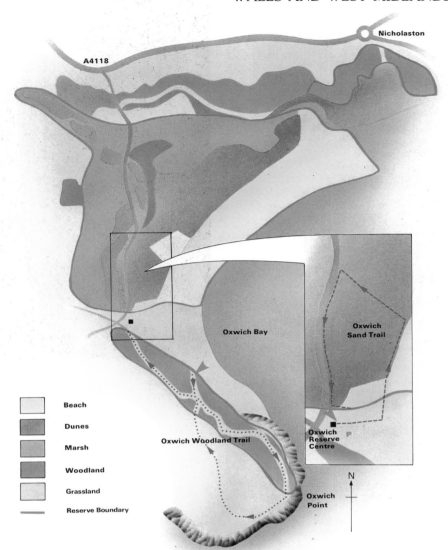

Beach

Dunes

Marsh

Woodland

Grassland

Reserve Boundary

Oxwich Bay

Oxwich Sand Trail

Oxwich Reserve Centre

Oxwich Woodland Trail

Oxwich Point

Nicholaston

A4118

The reason is apparently that the thin soil has the lime leached out of it by rain to a level lower than the heather roots. Birds you will see from this clifftop include the cormorant, gannet, redshank and oystercatcher. The return to the start is along the cliff and through woodlands which include a hazel coppice. In the Reserve Centre by the car park, the Nature Conservancy Council displays many of the interesting features of the trails and the work of the Council in studying the wildlife of the Reserve and combating erosion of the dune area – work in which you can play your part by sticking to the signed paths.

The Gower is a leisure paradise for the industrial towns of South Wales and its many beaches are often crowded in high season and at weekends. Swansea is the gateway to Gower, a busy city at the mouth of the Tawe or Swansea Valley. It was the world centre of the non-ferrous metal industry for almost a century, having many copper, zinc and nickel works clustered around the port and into the lower part of the valley. This industrial past is celebrated in a most unusual walking trail which takes in such curiosities as Europe's first reinforced concrete building (a grain mill of 1898), several ruined copper works and an industrial laboratory where the open hearth method of steel-making was perfected.

Porthcawl is a resort that grew to be a playground for both Swansea and Cardiff with safe bathing beaches and the vast funfair of Coney Beach. Porthcawl harbour is always busy with small craft and the pleasure trip boats that operate along the Bristol Channel coast. Royal Porthcawl is a championship golf course which no enthusiastic player should miss.

Anglers visiting the Gower area have a splendid choice of locations for shore fishing. Around Swansea the pier is noted for conger and winter whiting, while boat anglers out in the bay, to marks off the Mumbles, can expect bass, plaice, skate and monkfish. The fast currents around Oxwich attract big tope and the Port Eynon to Worms Head coast is excellent for bass. Outdoor types can camp in the heart of the Gower at Black Hills.

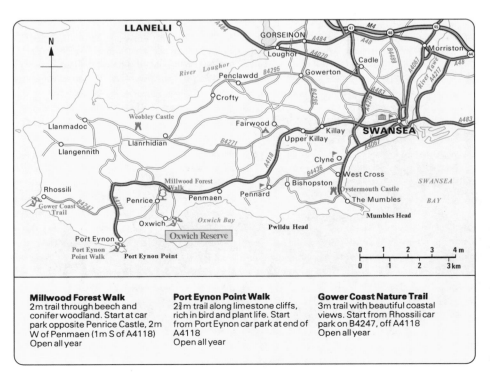

Millwood Forest Walk
2m trail through beech and conifer woodland. Start at car park opposite Penrice Castle, 2m W of Penmaen (1m S of A4118) Open all year

Port Eynon Point Walk
2½m trail along limestone cliffs, rich in bird and plant life. Start from Port Eynon car park at end of A4118 Open all year

Gower Coast Nature Trail
3m trail with beautiful coastal views. Start from Rhossili car park on B4247, off A4118 Open all year

Skomer Island Nature Trail

West Wales Naturalists' Trust,
7 Market Street, Haverfordwest,
Dyfed
Tel: Haverfordwest (0437) 5462

Reached by boat (April–October) from
Martin's Haven 2 miles past Marloes
village on unclassified road off B4327.
Also boats from Dale. Sailing details
from The Information Officer,
Pembrokeshire Coast National Park,
County Offices, Haverfordwest, Dyfed,
SA61 1QZ

Map references:
Martin's Haven SM760092
Skomer North Haven SM735095

4-mile trail around island Nature
Reserve with dramatic cliffs and
fascinating sea bird and seal populations

Facilities: Excellent descriptive and
illustrated guide, guided walks with
naturalist one day a week (details
National Park Offices and Trust). Note
sturdy footwear essential – boat landing
can be difficult, not suitable for
children under five or disabled people

The smallest of the National Parks in England
and Wales, no part of the Pembrokeshire Coast
Park is more than ten miles from the sea and
the majority of it falls within three miles from
the shore. It is a dramatic coast along which
the sea has carved the predominantly limestone and old red sandstone cliffs into a jagged-
ly indented shore which is the haven of a
raucous population of seabirds. Between the
jutting headlands are small bays with beaches
of wave-lapped sand. Here and there the sea
has battered away the soft rock into caves and
needle stacks, parting off small islands from
the mainland which are almost exclusively the
preserve of gulls, puffins, kittiwakes, gannets,
razorbills and fulmars.

Most of the islands can be visited but only
Caldey is permanently inhabited. Undisturbed
by man, plant and animal life develop a unique
balance, providing naturalists with unparal-
leled opportunities for the study of remote
habitats. A particularly active conservation
group, the West Wales Naturalists' Trust is
responsible for the tiny national Nature Reserve of Skomer Island, poised just a mile off
the mainland beyond the tiny islet of Midland
off Wooltack Point. Boats depart from Martin's Haven (two miles beyond the village of
Marloes) up to three times a day (not Mondays) landing at Skomer's North Haven. This
is a practical way of limiting the number of
people on the island at any one time to about a
hundred and minimising disturbance to the
environment. You are quite free to walk the
nature trail that circumnavigates Skomer's
cliffs by yourself but under the auspices of the

National Park authority there are also guided
tours led by a Naturalists' Trust expert that you
can join. To get to Skomer you will pay for a
boat ticket and a landing charge.

Skomer Reserve covers over 700 acres of
heath and rough fescue pastures reaching up to
200ft above sea level atop cliffs of a dark
volcanic basaltic rock. The remains of huts and
field enclosures show that Skomer was inhabited during the Iron Age and Norse visitors
named it Skalmey, a description of its near
disintegration into two islands at the narrow
rock bridge between the main part of Skomer
and The Neck. In the 18th century, the name
Skomer was current. Rabbits were farmed here
from the 14th century and some two centuries
later sheep and cattle were probably being
pastured here. There were sporadic attempts at
cultivation including quite expensive corn
growing during the mid-19th century and an
attempt at making early potatoes, brought on
by the generally mild climate, a paying crop in
the late Forties. The island was last farmed in
1949.

Skomer's trail starts on the cliff above the
warden's house overlooking the sheltered
North Haven, where puffins abound, and sets
off around the island's south cliffs. In the
South Haven, quickly reached over this narrow part of Skomer, is a cave where seals
retreat to breed. The clifftop gives a superb
view of the Pembroke Coast as far as St Ann's
Head, the turnpoint into Milford Haven. To
the south is the island of Skokholm, another
island managed by the Trust.

High Cliff is the first of the major sea bird
colonies reached on the walk – a tower of babel
with the kittiwakes occupying the lower storeys
of the rocks and guillemots and razorbills taking the higher ledges. The kittiwake is named
for the sound of its excited cry. Rock stacks are
a magnificent feature of this coastline and the
Mew Stone is among the largest. A buzzard
nests here, finding its food from the large

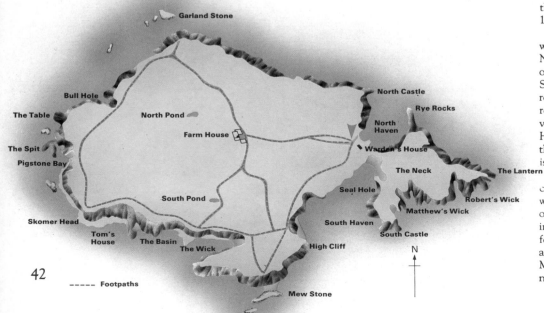

Stack Rocks near St Brides

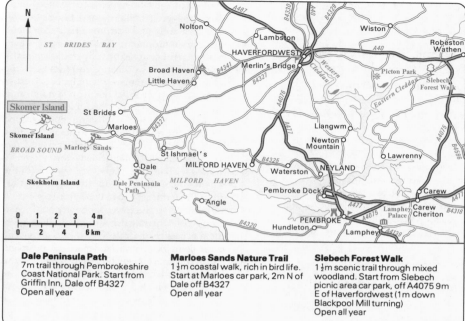

Dale Peninsula Path
7m trail through Pembrokeshire
Coast National Park. Start from
Griffin Inn, Dale off B4327
Open all year

Marloes Sands Nature Trail
1½m coastal walk, rich in bird life.
Start at Marloes car park, 2m N of
Dale off B4327
Open all year

Slebech Forest Walk
1½m scenic trail through mixed
woodland. Start from Slebech
picnic area car park, off A4075 9m
E of Haverfordwest (1m down
Blackpool Mill turning)
Open all year

population of smaller mammals on the island. The rabbit community has fluctuated in number over the years as waves of myxomatosis have taken their toll, but large numbers have survived. Skomer rabbits are a very mixed lot – wild races are interbred with various domestic types introduced over the years.

Quite the most intriguing of the five mammals native to the island is the Skomer vole, a relative of the bank vole found on the mainland. It is larger and lighter in colour and there are differences in its teeth and skull that make it a distinct island race. The common shrew, pygmy shrew and long-tailed field mouse complete Skomer's mammal population. All four small residents were probably introduced accidentally by visiting supply boats.

Skomer vegetation is subjected to many adverse influences. The rabbits can be very damaging and there are plots on the island enclosed to keep them out and study the ungrazed vegetation. The grass you will see is fescue but there are also large areas of heather grappling for survival in the face of the onslaught of bracken, and patches of the white-flowered sea campion. The vole inhabits sheltered areas with spring bluebells and, later, dense bracken cover. Other plants you may see are wood sage (it looks like garden sage), scarlet pimpernel, common sorrel and, in the marshy areas, silverweed and marsh cudweed. There is only one tree on the island, a black poplar standing in the yard of the ruined farmhouse buildings at the island's centre.

One of the best places to observe seals is at the island's most northerly point overlooking the offshore Garland Stone. Skomer is one of the most important grey seal-breeding grounds of this coast and up to a hundred pups are born here every year. Females give birth in September and October and feed the pups for only three weeks with a rich milk that fattens the baby rapidly. Pups are then left to moult off the white natal coat and learn to feed themselves before heading for the perils of the open sea.

Skomer's life isn't only above the waves. The waters around the island have been designated a Marine Reserve of four square miles in which observations of submarine life are being made and projects for the conservation of the underwater areas are pursued.

Back on the mainland you will find that warm sheltered bays and coves abound around St Brides Bay. Newgale sands are nearly two miles long but there are many smaller bathing beaches such as the sand and shingle of Porth Clais. Sailors and sightseers alike should head for the old smuggling village of Solva at the head of the flower-lined fjord of Gribin Cove, a National Trust property. Solva is a yachting harbour and a centre of crafts industries which include hand-made furniture and woollens.

Golfing fiends will find pleasant nine-hole courses at Milford Haven, Haverfordwest and Pembroke Docks. Fishing in the area is mainly sea or game, although coarse anglers at Bosherton Lakes, just north of St Govan's Head, have been rewarded by big catches of the shy tench. Sea fish in the bag locally are bass, pollack, mackerel, tope and conger taken from rock platforms or by beach casting. Shark boats sail out of Fishguard, a ferry port for Ireland – the picturesque lower town was the setting for Richard Burton's adaptation of Dylan Thomas's *Under Milk Wood*.

Pembrokeshire is not only the smallest National Park – it has Britain's smallest city. Enjoying this exalted status with its 12th–14th-century cathedral, St David's is in reality only a village. Poor drainage of the cathedral foundations has resulted in a tilt of the floor, a rise from west to east of three feet in the 298ft-long interior. St David's and the whole of the fascinating legend-ridden coastline of St Bride's Bay are a section of the 168-mile Pembrokeshire Coast Path, a feast of clifftop scenery and sea shore wildlife for the more ambitious walker.

Angling
River Cleddau
(Eastern): good for
sea trout June
onwards
Daily tickets (in
advance): Bush Inn,
Robeston Wathen
(near Narberth)
Tel: (0834) 860778
Water Authority:
WNWDA, Cambrian
Way, Brecon
Tel: (0874) 3181
Llys-y-Fran: large
reservoir for brown &
rainbow trout, 8m NE
of Haverfordwest off
B4329
Daily tickets: on-site
booth
Open Apr–Sep
Water Authority: as
River Cleddau
Milford Haven:
several miles of
deep-water fishing
for bass, ray, pollack
& whiting. Plus tope
& turbot by boat

Camping
Broadhaven:
Hasguard Cross
Caravan Park ►►►
Tel: (043 783) 443
Pleasant 25-pitch site
(no tents)
Open all year, must
book
Redlands Touring
Caravan Site ►►►
Level 60-pitch site
(no tents)
Open Apr–Sep, must
book Jul–Aug
Rosehill Country
Hotel Caravan
Park ►►
Sheltered 20-pitch
site (no tents)
Open Easter–Oct, no
bookings

Golfing
Haverfordwest:
Tel: (0437) 3565
Windy downland
course, 9 holes,
6258yds, par 69,

SSS70
Milford Haven:
Tel: (064 62) 2368
Parkland course 2m
N of town, 9 holes,
6024yds, par 70,
SSS69

General
Haverfordwest:
Haverfordwest
Castle, Museum, Art
Gallery & Record
Office: ruined 12th-
century stronghold,
formerly police HQ,
recently converted
Opening times vary
Tel: (0437) 3708
or Records Office)
3707
Lamphey: Lamphey
Palace: ruined 13th-
century residence of
early archbishops,
3m E of Pembroke
Open all year
Pembroke:
Pembroke Castle:
imposing 12th/13th-
century fortress
Open all year (ex Sun)
Tel: (064 63) 4585
Pembroke Motor
Museum: interesting
collection of old cars,
motor-cycles &
bicycles, 2m NW at
Pembroke Dock
Open Jun–Sep daily
10–6 (ex Sat)
Tel: (064 63) 3279
Picton: Picton Castle
Grounds & Graham
Sutherland Gallery:
many art exhibits plus
large shrub gardens
& woodland walks
Open (grounds)
Apr–Sep daily
10.30–6 (ex Mon &
Fri)
Tel: (043 786) 201
(gallery)
Easter–Sep
10.30–5.30 (ex Mon
& Fri), plus Sun 2–5 in
winter
Tel: (043 786) 296

Cwmrheidol Nature Trail

Central Electricity Generating Board, Rheidol Power Station, Capel Bangor, Aberystwyth, Dyfed

Tel: Capel Bangor (097 084) 667

On unclassified road 3 miles off A44 at Capel Bangor – signposted Cwmrheidol. Also access from Aberffrwd Halt on Vale of Rheidol Light Railway (BR, Aberystwyth – Devil's Bridge). Trail starts at CEGB visitor centre

Map reference: SN697797

2½-mile trail around a river valley dammed for a hydro-electric scheme – fascinating natural oak woodland, fish ladder and beautiful scenery

Facilities: Car parking; illustrated trail guide from Visitor Centre; exhibition about the hydro-electric scheme; power station tours

Rising on the boggy slopes of Plynlimon, source of the River Wye and River Severn, the River Rheidol has carved a magnificent valley through the mid-Wales hills on its short journey to the sea at Aberystwyth. The considerable energy of its fall from the mountains is harnessed in three stages by a remarkable hydro-electric scheme in which a chain of lakes has been created, culminating in the Cwmrheidol reservoir and power station deep in the heart of the beautiful Vale of Rheidol.

Around the reservoir, which is the final holding pond of the system, has been designed a nature trail which shows off the great sensitivity with which the scheme has been engineered and landscaped into this deep cleft. Dams, culverts, buildings and bridges are all built to a scale and with materials that blend into the environment very successfully – ever more so as the years go by. The trail starts at the power scheme's Visitor Centre, where the hydro-electric system which includes two other lakes some fifteen miles north on Plynlimon, is explained in a permanent exhibition.

Taking an anti-clockwise direction around the lake, the trail follows the road over the new Felin Newydd bridge, its abutments and terraces faced with multi-hued stones from a disused local quarry specially re-opened for the scheme's construction in the early Sixties. From the terraces, you may be able to see trout and salmon in the lower sanctuary pool. Migratory fish enter a fish lift here which gives them access to the reservoir waters above the main dam. A second ladder at the upstream end of the reservoir enables them to by-pass the Rheidol Falls and continue upriver to the gravel beds which are their spawning grounds.

As the trail leaves the road, it follows a track skirting the lower edge of the valley's wooded slopes. The woodland around Cwmrheidol is predominantly oak which was heavily cropped in the early part of this century. In a few places on both sides of the valley, the sessile oak (*Quercus petraea*, which flourishes in acid soils) has been supplanted by conifers such as the Japanese larch which is unusual in that it sheds its leaves in winter like a deciduous species.

The path shows an interesting mix of typical woodland ground flora and plants that inhabit the marshy meadow which falls away to the new lake. Bluebells shade the wood floor with a blue haze in the spring but the plants die back to leave the stage to wood sorrel, the buttercup, yellow flowers of the lesser celandine and the tiny green leaves of pignut (*Conopodium majus*). In the marshy areas you will see the spiked clumps of common rush, the mixed white and purple flowers of the tall, spiny marsh thistle and large moss clumps.

From this side of the reservoir, there is a good view of an area of wasteland high on the opposite valley side called The Stag. This is the spoil heap of a large lead mine – the seepage of poisonous metal salts from the waste rock prevents plant growth. The large number of lead mines in the Rheidol area used to pollute the river considerably and even today the CEGB has a small chemical plant to treat tributary stream water that runs off the spoil heaps. It actually removes the toxic elements.

Angling
Ponterwyd Lakes: a group of stillwaters 10m E of Aberystwyth containing brown & rainbow trout Daily tickets & Water Authority: as River Rheidol
River Rheidol: good brown trout, salmon & sea trout with ample access Daily tickets (in advance): J E Rosser, Queen Street, Aberystwyth *Tel: (0970) 617451* Water Authority: WNWDA, Cambrian Way, Brecon *Tel: (0874) 3181*
River Ystwyth: fair salmon & sea trout with good access Daily tickets & Water Authority: as River Rheidol

Camping
Aberystwyth: 'U' Tow Caravans Aberystwyth Holiday Village ▶ *Tel: (0970) 4211* Sloping 300-pitch site (50 tents) Open Apr–Oct, no bookings
Llandre: Riverside Park ▶▶▶ *Tel: (097 087) 682* Level site 4m E of Aberystwyth Open Easter & June–Sep

Golfing
Aberystwyth: *Tel: (0970) 2691*

Rolling meadowland course, 18 holes, 5735yds, par 67, SSS68
Borth & Ynyslas: *Tel: (097 081) 202* Windy links course, 18 holes, 5992yds, par 70, SSS70

General
Aberystwyth: Aberystwyth Castle: 13th-century ruins Open all year
National Library of Wales: impressive number of books, prints, MSS & drawings Open all year (ex Sun) *Tel: (0970) 3816/ 3819*
Machynlleth: Centre for Alternative Technology: displays of windpower, solar energy & vegetable growing, housed at old slate quarry Open all year daily 10–5 (or dusk in winter) *Tel: (0654) 2400*
Ponterwyd: Llywernog Silver Lead Mine: now converted into museum Open daily Easter–Sep
Tre'r Ddol: Yr Hen Gapel: museum depicting 19th-century religious life in Wales, 8m NE of Aberystwyth at A487/B4353 upper junction Open Apr–Sep daily 10–5 (ex Sun)

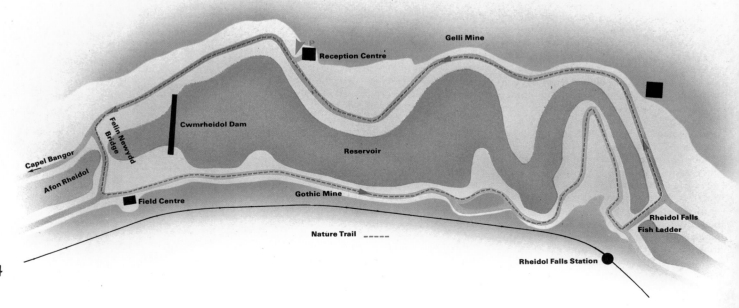

returns to the Visitor Centre past the power station which generates electricity from the water from Dinas Reservoir along the road.

The car is not the only way to visit Cwmrheidol – you can take the railway to Aberffrwd Halt from Aberystwyth station and enjoy, en route, the unique railway nature trail prepared by the West Wales Naturalists' Trust. A book describing the sights to be seen from the little steam line can be purchased at the main termini (the line ends at Devil's Bridge).

Now the local fishing association has stocked the Rheidol's water with both salmon and trout, the fishing is really looking up. Several sections of the river can be fished by visitors with a day ticket and the CEGB itself stocks and controls the waters of the Dinas and Nant-y-Moch reservoirs in the Rheidol headwaters. Aberystwyth is a major sea angling centre and the headquarters of the Shark Club of Wales.

The town is a sedate resort that has changed little this century. It is a university centre and is the location of the National Library of Wales where many rare books and documents can be viewed. There are campsites at Aberystwyth itself and four miles north east at Llandre.

Beaches along this part of the coast are fairly stony, although there are extensive sands at Borth, where the remains of a petrified forest can be seen at low tide. At the end of the beach is one of Wales' many small National Nature Reserves. The Ynyslas Reserve provides a fascinating seaside nature trail that would be a fitting contrast to the woodlands of Cwmrheidol for another day's outing.

Almost halfway along the southern section of the path is one of the older lead workings called the Gothic Mine. Little can be seen of the mine now except for a large bucket which was once a part of the ore transport system. Around the mine waste scree are the very old stumps (or 'stools') of oak from which new young growths have been generated. Depending on the size of timber required the trees were cropped in this way every fifty to a hundred years in those parts of the wood that were primitively managed.

The bark of the trees supports a fascinating flora of primitive organisms known as epiphytes. This is a group which includes mosses and liverworts. Some older trees have at least three epiphytic species clinging to them, each one settling in an area offering the particular blend of light exposure and moisture that it requires. Thus damp-seeking mosses will be at the base of the trunk and light-seeking ones on higher boughs. Ivy twines around the trees, offering, in its thicker clumps, a harbour for birds. There are several examples of trees bedecked with wild honeysuckle.

There is a considerable variety of bird life in the woods and the valley. Nest boxes have been posted throughout the woods to encourage the breeding of pied flycatchers – other insect feeders in the woods are tits, finches, warblers and the darting tree-creeper. Overhead you may be lucky enough to see the hovering buzzard, although a commoner sight is ravens and carrion crows. Down at the water's edge, mallards breed.

At the reservoir's north end, the trail follows the water edge and leads to a footbridge from which to see the tumble of the water over Rheidol Falls and a terrace to view the fish ladder. You may see fish in the water under the bridge preparing to make the leaps from pool to pool. Half way up the valley side, you can see the track of the 1ft 11in-gauge Rheidol light railway which marks, for the most part, the

boundary between the oak and the newer conifer woods. Around the bridge are many water-loving species on ground fed by spring water including water forget-me-not, bog stitchwort and marsh arrowgrass. The poisonous hemlock, water dropwort, is present here and close to the bridge are examples of the unusual, late-flowering western dwarf gorse. The trail

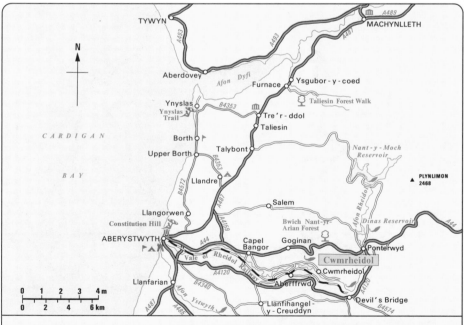

Bwlch Nant-yr-Arian Forest Visitor Centre
Numerous forest walks, rich in wildlife. Entrance 3m W of Ponterwyd off A44
Open Easter–Oct 10–5 (until 7 Jul–Aug)

Constitution Hill Nature Trail
3m clifftop walk with fine views.
Start at foot of Constitution Hill, Aberystwyth
Open all year

Taliesin Forest Walk
1m wooded trail through Artist's Valley. Start at Forest Office 1m E of Furnace (7m SW of Machynlleth) off A487
Open all year

Ynyslas Nature Trail
1½m walk through dunes & flora.
Start at Information Kiosk, Borth (7m N of Aberystwyth)
Open all year

Penrhos Nature Reserve Trail

Anglesey Aluminium Metal Ltd,
Penrhos Nature Reserve,
Holyhead, Gwynedd
Tel: Holyhead (0407) 2522

On A5 2 miles east of Holyhead at west end of Stanley Embankment

Map reference: SH275805

2¼-mile trail around coastal headland Nature Reserve – large sea bird population

Facilities: Trail brochures and illustrated sign boards on trail; car park; picnic area; tea cabin; exhibition; bird and animal hospital; good facilities for disabled

In Welsh, Anglesey is celebrated as the Mam Cymru, Mother of Wales, for its fertility and production of corn for both the native inhabitants and the Romans who knew this island as Mona. Separated from the Welsh mainland by, at some points only 200 yards of treacherous water, the Menai Straits, this island has played a dominant role in the history of Britain. It was from here that Owain Tudor came, the Welsh squire whose grandson defeated Richard III at Bosworth Field to become Henry VII and found the Tudor dynasty. Not only was Mona rich in agriculture but the island had valuable minerals and copper ores. It is an irony that the great Parys Mountain copper mine was closed by its inability to compete with imported copper mined by, among others, Rio Tinto Zinc who, in partnership with Kaiser Aluminium, have built the Penrhos aluminium smelter on Holy Island.

The companies bought the land of the large Penrhos Estate, a holding which included the foreshore of Beddmanarch Bay and some former shooting lands. These are sited each side of the A5 at the point where it crosses Telford's embankment (actually called Stanley embankment after the one-time owners of

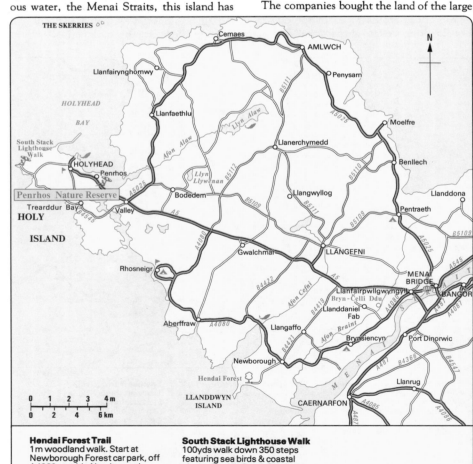

Angling

River Cefni: good trout with occasional salmon

Free fishing (with prior permission of local farmers) Water Authority: WNWDA (Gwynedd River Division), Cambrian Way, Brecon *Tel: (0874) 3181*

Holyhead: fishing from pier & breakwater for ray & tope. Good deep-sea fishing beyond ten miles

Tackle shop: Jay's Fishing Parlour, 16 Newry Street, Holyhead *Tel: (0407) 4171*

Llyn Alaw: large reservoir 9m E of Holyhead at Llanerchymedd offering excellent brown & rainbow trout

Daily tickets: on-site office (Apr–Sep) Water Authority: as River Cefni

Camping

Brynsiencyn: Fron Farm ▶▶ *Tel: (024873) 310* Small 79-pitch site (40 tents) 6m SW of Menai Bridge off A4080 Open Apr–Sep, must book Jul–Aug

Pentraeth: Rhos Caravan Park ▶ *Tel: (024870) 214* Well-kept 100-pitch site (50 tents) Open Mar–Oct, must book Jul–Aug

Rhosneigr: Bodfan Farm ▶ *Tel: (0407) 810563* Gently sloping 96-pitch site (60 tents) 8m SE of Holyhead Open Apr–Sep, must book

Golfing

Anglesey (Rhosneigr): *Tel: (0407) 810219* Easily walked links course, 18 holes, 5700yds, par 68, SSS67

Holyhead: *Tel: (0407) 3279* Treeless seaside course, 18 holes, 6081yds, par 71, SSS70

Riding

Benllech: Benllech Riding Stables (A J Hewitt), Benllech Bay (8m N of Menai Bridge) *Tel: (024874) 2345*

General

Beaumaris: Beaumaris Castle: early 14th-century moated fortress Open all year

The Tudor Rose: restored 15th-century building housing regular art exhibitions Open Jul–mid-Sep daily 10.30–5.30, plus off-season by request *Tel: (0248) 810203*

Llanfairpwllgwyll: Bryn-Celli-Ddu: excavated archaeological site 4m SW of Menai Bridge off A4080 Accessible all year

Plas Newydd: 18th-century house with fine views & gardens Open Apr–Oct daily 12.30–5.30 (ex Sat) *Tel: (0248) 714795*

Menai Bridge: Museum of Childhood: many rare dolls, toys & games plus art gallery Open Easter–Oct daily 10–6 (Sun 1–5), plus winter opening by appointment *Tel: (0248) 712498*

Hendai Forest Trail
1m woodland walk. Start at Newborough Forest car park, off A4080 outside Newborough Open all year

South Stack Lighthouse Walk
100yds walk down 350 steps featuring sea birds & coastal plants. Start at South Stack Lighthouse, 3m W of Holyhead Open May–mid-July

Penrhos) to Holy Island. The vision and energy of one man has made this headland and the west shore of the inland sea formed by the embankment into a Nature Reserve which attracts thousands of birds of some 150 species. Once a full-time policeman, Ken Williams, MBE, recently retired to devote all his energy to the administration and upkeep of the Reserve he envisaged in 1971 and saw through to reality with the help of local volunteers. Practically, Mr Williams, now the Reserve director, has separated the functions of the lands into the two natural halves dictated by the route of the A5 and the main railway line.

To the south of the road is about a hundred acres of salt marsh and scrub bordering the inland sea. This is dedicated to the delicate work of fostering colonies of terns and other birds of the fringe between the land and sea. Over 500 pairs of terns nest on the emergent islands of the sheltered sea and one such group is known to contain four species of this bird; the common, roseate, arctic and sandwich terns. A Penrhos arctic tern set a world record for bird migration when it was captured 14 000 miles away in New South Wales, Australia. The specialist conservation area is only open to ornithologists with the director's permission.

It is to the Reserve's northern half, with road access from the A5, that the public flock. As Williams himself says, 'This part of the reserve is managed for both people and plants and animals'. Around its perimeter runs a two-and-a-quarter mile nature trail that takes in the seashore and some of the Reserve's woodlands. The heart of the public Penrhos area can also be explored by the many walks that have been created through the woods of spruce, cypress, oak, sycamore and chestnut.

The Penrhos Nature Reserve Trail starts at the central cluster of buildings in an area entered by an unusual gate. It was found during the massive clean-up campaign which was required to establish the reserve and is thought to be an original Telford Toll gate. The A5 at this point was one of the last trunk roads in Britain to be subject to a private toll. The buildings include a bird and animal hospital where Ken Williams and his assistant wardens take in injured animals from all over north Wales and the north west of England.

Young birds that have not reached maturity before being prematurely ejected from nests by tree-felling or building work are frequent patients but a badger has been nursed back to health here after a hit-and-run car accident. Rarer birds rescued by the hospital include the peregrine falcon, gyr falcon and snowy owl. Some of the recovered patients are kept in enormous aviaries in the woods – you may see snowy owls and eagle owls in them. Birds recuperate in fifteen smaller cages, some of them heated by infra red lamps. Another building in the central area is the nature room, with its exhibits of work on the Reserve and some of the trail's more interesting features.

Along the trail, large chart noticeboards describe the flora and fauna you are likely to find. An interesting idea is that some of them are changed at intervals, so the information reflects specimens you will see in a particular

season. Among the boards are those describing plants and trees – wild cyclamen is a rarity growing here – butterflies and, of course, the Reserve's forte, birds of the sea and shore.

The Penrhos emblem is that charming orangy red-billed wader, the oystercatcher, resident here all year round. Other natives on the rocky shore of Beddmanarch Bay are redshanks, ringed plovers, shelducks and the rarer red-breasted merganser. Colder weather brings with it the huge flocks of migrants which depend on salt marshes for winter feeding on arthropods and other small sea creatures. Among less common visitors have been whimbrel, black-tailed godwit, the Slavonian grebe and greenshank.

Two freshwater ponds, the Lily Pond near the car park and the Scouts Pond deeper in the Reserve, are populated by introduced gaggles of geese, among them the grey lag and barnacle species, and some common and ornamental ducks. You may see the eider duck in both fresh and saltwater locations. These colonies have attracted both native and migrant species to these restored habitats.

While it is the Anglesey Aluminium Metal Company that owns the land at Penrhos, the work is funded from its own resources. No charge is made for admission but to enjoy the wildlife here, a donation is a small price to pay.

Penrhos is on Holy Island separated from the main island of Anglesey by a narrow marshy channel. Holyhead, at the end of the A5, two miles on from the Reserve is a busy ferry port for Ireland and an industrial centre with a Roman fort, many seaside attractions and a shingle beach. Tankers and bauxite ore-carriers for the aluminium works can be seen mooring and entering port. The furthest west reach of Anglesey and Holy Island is the South Stack lighthouse built in 1808. Reached by a footpath over a narrow bridge, the lighthouse can be visited and enables you to view a considerable population of cliff-nesting birds.

To Holyhead

Cypress Walk

Chestnut Walk

Four Gates Walk

Conant's Walk

Scouts Pond

Nature Room

Director's House

Ellens Walk

Hospital

Telford Gate

Stanley Walk

Grace's Pond

Beddmanarch Bay

To Bangor

Lily Pond

Telford Toll House

Trail - - - - -

Anglesey's main island has a curious topography of shallow valleys in ranks with low hills – undulations that are parallel to the Menai Straits. These are like the fading ripples of the great upthrust of land forming the Snowdon range which can be seen in the distance from many points on the island. Evidence of the island's history from Roman times is prolific. Most majestic of all is Beaumaris Castle, the last of Edward I's great fortifications blocking the opposite end of the Menai Straits from Caernarfon. The castle was never completely finished. The town, a small resort and sailing centre, takes its unusual name from the marsh drained to make the castle moat – *Beau Marais*. Plas Newydd, to the south end of the Menai Straits and opposite the wooded grounds of Vaynol Hall on the mainland, is National Trust property which was once the seat of the Marquess of Anglesey (the 1st Marquess led the cavalry at Waterloo). The fine 18th-century mansion contains a considerable number of Whistler paintings, period furniture and a military museum.

Campers will find the island has a fairly mild climate and has some meadow sites and one seaside location that are considerably less exposed than the mountain sites of Snowdonia, which is still within an hour's drive. If you would like to combine some angling with your visit to the Penrhos Reserve, Len Williams welcomes shore fishermen who want an exciting day hunting bass, mullet, cod and whiting.

Snowdonia: Miners' Track and Cwm Idwal Trails

Nature Conservancy Council, Penrhos Road, Bangor, Gwynedd LL57 2LQ

Tel: Bangor (0248) 4001

The Miners' Track
On A4086 in Llanberis Pass 1 mile from junction with A498 (Pen y Gwryd Hotel)

Map reference: SH648557

3-mile section of public footpath leading to Snowdon summit through glacial valley with lakes, mineral workings and rock and bog vegetation

Facilities: Car park (often crowded, early start advisable); illustrated trail leaflet from the Council and National Park Visitor Centres (nearest in Llanberis); cafeteria and Youth Hostel at start of path

Cwm Idwal Trail
Off A5 at Ogwen Cottage Mountain School – west end of Llyn Ogwen

Map reference: SH648603

2-mile trail around small lake in the floor of a glacial valley under spectacular rock crags and slabs – sheep grazing experiments on view

Facilities: Small car park at Ogwen Cottage; illustrated trail leaflet from Council or National Park Visitor Centres

---

The horseshoe tiara of the principal Snowdon peaks surmounted by Yr Wyddfa, the summit itself, is at the heart of some of the most spectacular mountains in Britain. It is a land deeply gouged by glacial action some 10 000–12 000 years ago and an environment that continues to change under the influences of water and frost, combined with both the industrial and leisure activities of man. Copper and slate have been mined and quarried in the shadow of the principal peaks by hardened men whose homes lay several miles away on the valley floors. Early in the days of electricity generation, the tremendous rainfall of the area was recognised as a useful energy source and a lake high on Snowdon was tapped to drive hydro-electric turbines.

The principal industry was and is agriculture, the grim struggle of the hill sheep-farmer to foster his flock in the teeth of the elements. Just as sheep gnawing at the thin vegetation have changed the face of Snowdon so have men's feet. Thousands of tourists every year contribute to erosion of the main paths to the summit, one of the most pronounced symptoms of the pressures leisure activities generate on the countryside.

All this activity, stretching back over the centuries has wrought its change on the area's animal and plant life. Both flora and fauna have a precarious existence at best on the thin soils of powdered rhyolite rocks and the poor nutrient properties of this material. The exposure, too, affects plant life and so the net result is that much of the vegetation of the higher slopes has an alpine character. The two main selected trails show a wide selection of the effects all these factors have on wildlife and plants in Snowdonia, while the Gwydr Forest Trail is, in contrast, a look at modern afforestation which makes considerable commercial advantage of otherwise unviable land.

The Miners' Track forms a part of one of the main walkers' routes up Snowdon. It is a wide stone path starting from the car park at Pen-y-Pass Youth Hostel (at the head of the Llanberis Pass) and, rising some 750ft over a distance of about five miles, it reaches Llyn Glaslyn, a small blue lake set in the bowl of the high peaks. Like Cwm Idwal, the second of the trails, this is one of the sixteen National Nature Reserves designated by the Nature Conservancy Council within the Snowdonia National Park. The first three miles of the track have been marked with carved slate numbers corresponding to points of interest in the trail booklet (available from the Council or the Llanberis Visitor Centre). The nature trail ends at the causeway across Llyn Llydaw built, like the track itself, to aid the removal of copper ore from the mines around the lakes during the mid-19th century. Trail followers must wear robust walking shoes, preferably giving ankle protection and carry an extra warm garment – a lightweight waterproof is an advisable item.

The rocks that confront you as you set out from the car park are typical of the Snowdon outcrop, the rhyolite of what is geologically known as a syncline. This is a rock bed, folded as it has emerged from the sea, the downward layers of the giant ripple. As the glaciers bore down on these rocks with their load of frozen-in stone teeth, they were ground to the powder which forms today's soil. Mat grass (*Nardus stricta*), well-adapted to the poor soil and constant sheep-nibbling is the dominant species

Swallow Falls, Betws-y-Coed

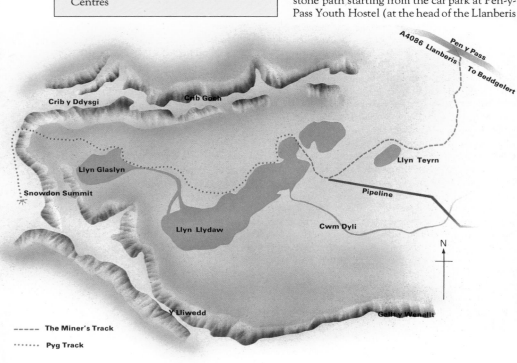

- - - - - The Miner's Track

· · · · · Pyg Track

Crib y Ddysgi
Crib Goch
A4086 Llanberis
Pen y Pass
To Beddgelert
Llyn Teyrn
Llyn Glaslyn
Pipeline
Snowdon Summit
Cwm Dyli
Llyn Llydaw
N
Y Lliwedd
Gallt y Wenallt

here. There are other rocks along the trail, particularly the volcanic pumice tuff which breaks down to provide a more nutritious soil supporting the preferred (by sheep!) fescue, bent grass, wild thyme and the yellow flowered tormentil (*Potentilla erecta*).

The path is a steady climb and as you get higher, you can look down into the Nant Gwynant valley which is quite densely wooded in parts. Almost certainly in the past, oak, birch, beech and ash woods cloaked the mountain's lower slopes reaching as high as 1500–1600ft where stumps have been found preserved in peat. Now the tree line is considerably lower than this because in recent times, tree regeneration has been prevented by sheep grazing. Even so, you may be able to pick out the odd stunted tree on ledges which are inaccessible to animals – rowan in particular survives in this way, since its seeds are carried to high points by birds.

The first, small lake you come across is Llyn Teyrn, below the path on the glacial valley floor. It has escaped the poisoning by copper which makes the two upper lakes so barren and small brown trout breed here. The valley is called Cwm Dyli and it contains several ruined buildings. The one on the lake shore was probably a miner's barracks but other ruins are traces of the old farming system still used in the Alps. These were the bothies (or *hafod* in

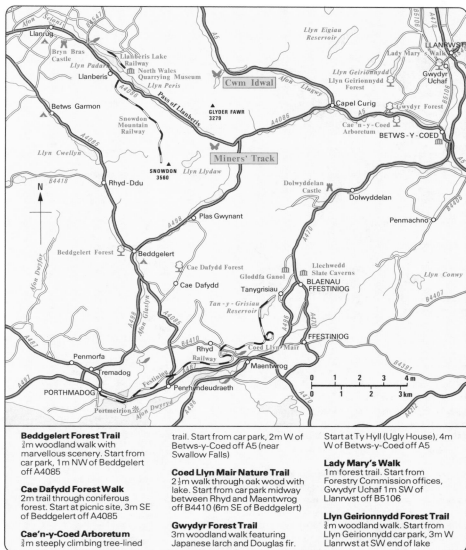

Beddgelert Forest Trail
¾m woodland walk with marvellous scenery. Start from car park, 1m NW of Beddgelert off A4085

Cae Dafydd Forest Walk
2m trail through coniferous forest. Start at picnic site, 3m SE of Beddgelert off A4085

Cae'n-y-Coed Arboretum
¾m steeply climbing tree-lined

trail. Start from car park, 2m W of Betws-y-Coed off A5 (near Swallow Falls)

Coed Llyn Mair Nature Trail
2½m walk through oak wood with lake. Start from car park midway between Rhyd and Maentwrog off B4410 (6m SE of Beddgelert)

Gwydyr Forest Trail
3m woodland walk featuring Japanese larch and Douglas fir.

Start at Ty Hyll (Ugly House), 4m W of Betws-y-Coed off A5

Lady Mary's Walk
1m forest trail. Start from Forestry Commission offices, Gwydyr Uchaf 1m SW of Llanrwst off B5106

Llyn Geirionnydd Forest Trail
¾m woodland walk. Start from Llyn Geirionnydd car park, 3m W Llanrwst at SW end of lake

Welsh) of the shepherds grazing their sheep on the mountains in summer and retreating to the home farm or *hendre* for the winter.

Much of the ground round here is peat bog formed as layers of grass and moss are deposited under conditions of high rainfall and poor drainage. Plants typical of this altitude and the wet acid conditions are mosses and two peculiarities of the plant world, the butterwort and sundew (*Drosera rotundifolia*). These both digest insects trapped in a thick enzyme glue on their leaves – a neat piece of adaptation to supplement the thin diet. Another inhabitant of the peat bog is the fern-like club moss with its long tendrils like the branches of a fir tree.

After Llyn Teyrn you begin the climb up to Llyn Lydaw, parallel with the twin steel pipe of the Cwm Dyli hydro-electric scheme still in operation today some seventy-five years after its opening. This middle lake, with a depth of about 180ft, is dammed naturally by a rock step ground to a lip by the glacier. Owing to the high rainfall (up to 200 inches of water a year) and the sporadic power station demands, the lake level varies considerably and the causeway may be water-covered.

Much of the lake shore is infertile due to the

high copper content of the water which receives the washings from the mine tailings. However, since the activities of the ore-crushing plant stopped in 1916, the copper level is dropping and it is hoped to see a lot more plant and insect life establish itself in and around the water. There are many signs of glacial action here, with pavement stones scored by ice-trapped boulders and moraine humps caused by the dumping of debris as the ice melted. Here is the place to have a rest and watch out for the unusual chough, a crow with sleek black colouring and characteristic red legs. Other birds of the Snowdon valleys are the raven, the tiny meadow pipit and the carrion crow.

The energetic will carry on for Snowdon's summit past Llyn Glaslyn and up a scree scramble to the zig-zag section of the Pen-y-Gwryd (Pyg) Track, quite a severe last section which should not be attempted in anything other than climbing or walking boots.

Why not save your strength for the splendour of the Cwm Idwal Nature Reserve trail which displays another facet of the Snowdonia mountain's many attractions? The trail through the Reserve is reached by footpath

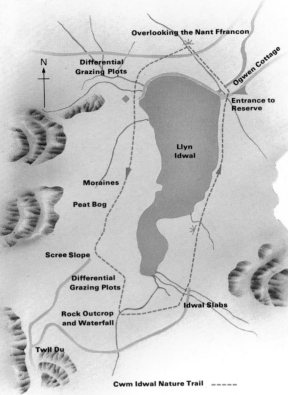

Overlooking the Nant Ffrancon

N

Differential
Grazing Plots

Ogwen Cottage

Entrance to
Reserve

Llyn
Idwal

Moraines

Peat Bog

Scree Slope

Differential
Grazing Plots

Idwal Slabs

Rock Outcrop
and Waterfall

Twll Du

Cwm Idwal Nature Trail — — — —

species typical of the habitat, such as the marsh cinquefoil and bogbean.

Cwm Idwal is a valley of rocks, too. The boulders tumbling down from the Devil's Kitchen (Twll Du) make a scree which harbours plants that have established themselves out of the way of grazing sheep. You will see that on newly-disturbed or fallen rock it is the lichens that have taken over. As these plants decay and other seed and rock dust is blown here, a thin soil develops. In the long-established areas, you may find bilberry and

from the Ogwen Cottage Mountain School (which has a small car park) off the main A5 some five-and-a-half miles from Capel Curig (about ten miles from The Miners' Track). The gate to the partially fenced area is about half a mile from the road.

Cwm Idwal ('cwm' is Welsh for valley) is a glacial valley about 1000ft above sea level lying under the black peak of Tryfan and the spectacular rock cleft of the Devil's Kitchen. The ground is part of the National Trust's extensive holdings in Snowdonia and the Reserve area is leased to the trail designers, the Nature Conservancy Council. Making a circuit around the lake in the valley floor of about two miles, the path takes in several viewpoints and some fascinating experiments on the effects grazing animals have had on the vegetation.

Sheep have not only reduced the woodland over much of the Welsh mountains. Their grazing has also changed the whole nature of the moorland across which they feed. As the Cwm Idwal experiments with enclosures to keep sheep out of certain areas show, heather, ling and purple moor grass quickly spring back again to form the natural ground cover. As it is, the vegetation is very similar to that of the Miners' Track — mat grass in the poorer soil areas and bent grass and sheep fescue in those areas where the soil conditions are a little more alkaline.

Like most glacial lakes, Llyn Idwal is quite shallow — maximum 36ft depth — and it has become silted and bedded with mud and peat. Unlike the lakes of the Miners' Track, there have been no mineral workings in this area and the water is a breeding ground for minnow and trout which are preyed upon by gulls, occasional cormorants and herons. Observers say that whooper swans overwinter here. Around the lake shore are extensive boggy areas supporting

Angling
River Dwyryd: good salmon & sea trout Jun–Oct
Daily tickets: Grapes Hotel, Maentwrog *Tel: (076 685) 208*
Water Authority: WNWDA, Cambrian Way, Brecon *Tel: (0874) 3181*
River Glaslyn: very good sea trout
Daily tickets: Saracen's Head, Beddgelert *Tel: (076 686) 223*
Water Authority: as River Dwyryd
River Seiont: good salmon in May plus brown trout
Daily tickets: D Huxley-Jones, 3 Penrallt, Caernarfon *Tel: (0286) 3186*
Water Authority: as River Dwyryd
Porthmadog: Traeth Bach estuary for bass, flounder & plaice. Boat fishing for most flatfish
Tackle shop: The Angling Centre, 11 High Street, Porthmadog *Tel: (0766) 2464*

Camping
Beddgelert: Snowdonia Forest Park Camping Ground ▶
Tel: (076 686) 288
Partly sloping 280-pitch site (140 tents) Open Apr–Oct, no bookings
Bethesda: Ogwen Bank Caravan Park ▶▶▶
Tel: (0248) 600486
Partly sloping 30-pitch site (no tents) Open Mar–Oct, must book Jul–Aug
Betws Garmon: Bryn Gloch Farm Caravan & Camping Park ▶▶▶
Tel: (028 685) 216
Well-kept 80-pitch site (20 caravans) Open Mar–Oct, must book
Llanrug: Tyn-y-Coed Camping Site ▶▶
Tel: (0286) 3565
Partly sloping 60-pitch site (20 caravans) Open May–Sep, must book Jul–Aug
Llandwrog: White Tower Caravan Park ▶
Tel: (0286) 830649
Grassy 12-pitch site (no tents) Open mid-May–Sep, must book Jul–Aug

Golfing
Caernarfon: *Tel: (0286) 3783*
Parkland course 2m S of Caernarfon off A499, 9 holes, 2768yds, SSS67
Porthmadog: *Tel: (0766) 2037*
Links course with good views, 18 holes, 5600yds, par 68, SSS67

General
Betws-y-Coed: Conwy Valley Railway Museum: comprehensive displays & exhibits from the North Wales railways
Open Easter–Sep daily 10.30–5.30 (plus weekends in Oct)
Tel: (069 02) 568
Blaenau Ffestiniog: Gloddfa Ganol: mountain tourist centre including slate mine site, museum & play area
Open Easter–Oct 10–5.30 daily
Tel: (076 681) 664
Caernarfon: Caernarfon Castle: 13th/14th-century fortress, scene of Prince Charles' investiture
Open all year
Dolwyddelan: Dolwyddelan Castle: restored 12th-century keep with curtain walls, 5m SW of Betws-y-Coed off A496
Open all year
Llanberis: North Wales Quarrying Museum: foundry mill, machinery & workshop
Open Easter–Sep daily 9.30–7
Snowdon Mountain Railway: 2½hr runs to top of Mount Snowdon
Open Apr–Sep daily
Llanrug: Bryn Bras Castle & Grounds: early Victorian castle with beautiful gardens
Open May–Sep daily (ex Sat) 1–5 (10.30–5 Jul–Aug)
Tel: (028 682) 210
Porthmadog: Festiniog Railway: historic narrow-gauge railway re-opened by enthusiasts
Daily service Mar–Nov, for timetable information
Tel: (0766) 2384

heather. The great Idwal Slabs which you pass on the homeward leg of the trail are a Mecca for rock climbers who form queues to climb them at peak times. Other climbers that you may spot are wild (feral) goats which have bred from escaped domestic animals.

The last leg of the trail follows the lake shore and passes a small rocky island a few yards off shore. Its proud crown of shrubs and plants is a final reminder that where sheep do not stray, the vegetation is that much more varied.

Variety is what the Forestry Commission have tried to provide in the replanting of the woods around Ty Hyll (the Ugly House) on the A5 between Betws-y-Coed and Capel Curig. A three-mile trail, the Gwdyr Forest Trail, starting 200 yards behind the quaint landmark cottage takes you high into new mixed deciduous and coniferous woodlands, much of it planted since 1956. The predominant deciduous tree is beech but most commercial conifers, including the Christmas tree, Norwegian spruce, are shown in this wood, which was at one time one of the Commission's foremost tree nurseries. The trail leads downhill into the valley of the River Llugwy above Swallow Falls and back to the start car park via an old lead mine, the haunts of ravens and buzzards and examples of modern forestry techniques.

Deep in the heart of another forest, at Beddgelert, is one of the major campsites in the area. Run by the Forestry Commission, this site in the valley between Moel Hebog and Snowdon is a beautiful setting for the outdoor life — and the woods around the site are laced with nature trails, too.

Snowdonia is a vast outdoor pursuits park which can provide pony-trekking, canoeing, fishing, orienteering, rock-climbing and even sailing to visitors. It is a land for the sightseer. There are three little train lines in the northern part of the National Park and one runs on Snowdon itself. The Mountain Railway has a track from Llanberis to the summit of Snowdon which could provide an easy route down for weary nature trailers. An even longer rail trip is the Festiniog Railway's line from Porthmadog, an old slate port, up to the quarry town of Blaenau Ffestiniog — the line stops at Tanygrisiau, which is a few miles short of the original terminal.

Wales' north and west coasts are not far from the heart of Snowdonia — families will find all the fun of the fair at Llandudno. There are much quieter charms in the Victorian resort of Criccieth and the regional centre of Caernarfon, its castle standing guard over the Menai Straits. Both Conwy, at the Conwy river mouth, and Llandudno have superb links golf courses — the Caernarvonshire at Conwy and the North Wales at Llandudno face each other across the estuary.

Most of all, Snowdonia is the country of the walker. You can choose to be as lazy or as energetic as you wish — striding the mountain tops or following the courses of old railways on the valley floor. The scenic beauty and mountain grandeur you encounter on the selected trails will almost certainly whet your appetite for a return, and perhaps some more ambitious recreation.

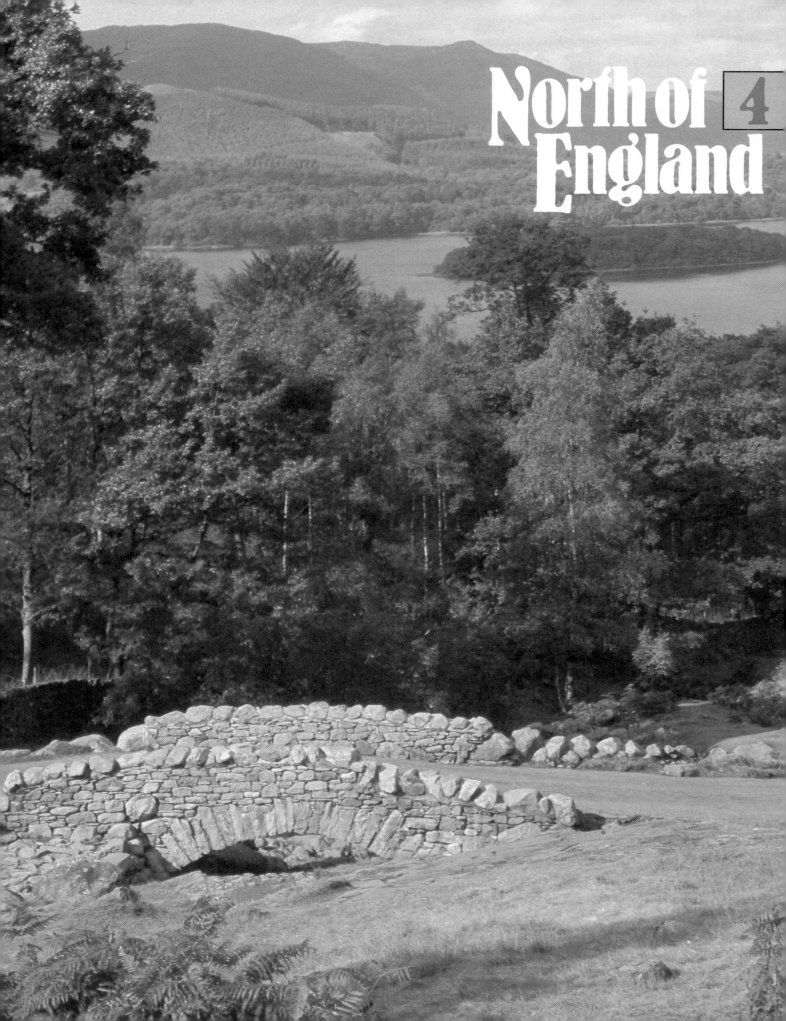

Capesthorne Hall Trail

Capesthorne, Macclesfield,
Cheshire, SK11 9JY
Tel: Chelford (0625) 861221

On A34 1 mile south of junction with
A537–5½ miles west of Macclesfield, 6
miles north of Congleton

Map reference: SJ845728

Approximately 1-mile trail around the
landscaped grounds of early 18th-
century hall which has an ornamental
lake and a varied flora and fauna

Facilities: Trail leaflet; car park; crafts,
gifts and souvenir shops; gardens

Where the peaks of Derbyshire tumble to the
great plain of Cheshire a town grew up which
was to establish itself as a silk-weaving centre
known throughout the world. Macclesfield
still has a small silk industry concentrating on
the high-value markets for silk scarves and
head squares which are both made and printed
locally. A town of steep streets, it is edged on
its western side by a rich meadowland of dairy
farms among which are to be found several
stately homes, evidence of the area's once great
affluence.

One such mansion is Capesthorne, home of
the Capesthornes, Wards and, today's descen-
dants, the Bromley-Davenports, since before
the Norman Conquest. Capesthorne's name is
derived from Old Norse describing a thorn
bush on the scene of a battle. To commemorate this, a new plantation of hawthorns was
sited near the Dew Pond in the gardens in
1967. Around the hall's extensive gardens and
ornamental pools and lake, the Cheshire Conservation Trust has designed a one-mile nature
trail which demonstrates the natural harmony
between the work of 18th-century landscape
gardeners and wild plants and flowers.

The trail begins through the gardens to the
left of the hall, built in 1722 close to a stand of
lime trees which produce a pale, hard wood,
once used to carve the intricate printing blocks
used in Macclesfield's silk industry. You will
also see the hall's chapel, still in use, which was
once thought to be the work of John Wood of
Bath but which is now identified as more likely
to have been built by William Smith of Wergs,
Staffordshire. To the right of the path before
the chapel, is an unusual pine tree that has
tufts of three needles, an example of *Pinus
ponderosa*. Other trees near the chapel gates are
English yew, a shade-loving tree very often
found in churchyards because its seed is surrounded by a fleshy red cup and the foliage is
poisonous to cattle. Cattle are therefore dis-
couraged from entering church grounds. There
are also some specimens of *Wellingtonia* here,
relatives of the American *Sequoia*, their rough
bark the haunt of insect-catching treecreepers
which have the amusing habit of circling the
tree in a spiral, then flying down to start again
when they reach the top.

Capesthorne has a good balance between
native trees and beautiful and more exotic
species—landscapers prized the coloured
foliage and the seasonal changes of colour that
would contrast with British trees. Of five oak
species in the park, you will see the common
pedunculate oak, *Quercus robur*, the evergreen
holm oak, *Quercus ilex*, and the sessile or
durmast oak, *Quercus petraea*, all natives. The
aliens are the red oak, *Quercus borealis* and
Spanish oak, a cross that retains the furry acorn

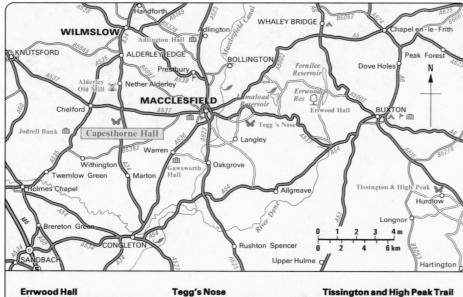

cups of the far-distant parent Turkey oak.

As you leave the chapel and pass the tennis
courts, you will be on your way to the lakes and
ponds formed by the damming of the Fanshawe
Brook, a tiny stream also put to use by two
other local halls. The ponds and lakes (Capesthorne also owns the much larger nearby Redesmere) teem with water life. Fish species here
include roach, the fighting perch and bream as
well as the larger specimens, carp and the
predatory pike. If you are lucky, you may see
the shy vegetarian water vole, which lives in
holes in the bank of the main lake. Water birds
nest here. Whereas the woodlands of Capesthorne echo to the sounds of woodpeckers and
nuthatches, and the quick flight of a wren or
spotted flycatcher surprises the eye, the water
is the province of grebes, mallards, coots and
moorhens. In the lake fringes and cover of
sedge and rushes is the reed bunting.

Most of the movement in the water is caused
by the insect population. Pond skaters utilise
the water's surface tension to skid across and
break up the mirror of the lake. Water boat-
men and great diving beetles have the trick of
trapping air bubbles from the surface which
they carry underwater, enabling them to stay
below for several minutes at a time. In late
spring and early summer only, you might see
the newts in and around the water searching
out breeding places. For the rest of the year,
these amphibians inhabit damp shady ground-
stalking insects and grubs, hibernating in winter. Grass snakes grow to a considerable
size—about 3-feet long is common—and they

Errwood Hall
1½m woodland walk with picnic
area. Start 4m NW of Buxton off
A5002 near Errwood Reservoir
Open all year

Tegg's Nose
Walk over escarpment. Start 2mE
of Macclesfield on unclassified
road off A537. Car park
Open all year

Tissington and High Peak Trail
Numerous walks along the old
Buxton to Ashbourne railway.
Start at Hurdlow, 6m SE of
Buxton off A515
Open all year

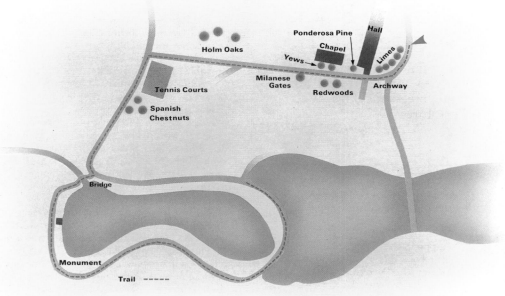

are Britain's largest native snake. They feed on small reptiles and swim in much the same way as they travel across land—with a snaking action.

Plants of the lake fringe display the gradient of the bank under the water. Water lilies, of which Capesthorne's lake has both the white and yellow varieties, float their pads over the deeper water, a little nearer in you find mares-tail, *Hippurus vulgaris*, in purple and green-leaved stalks and as the land begins to emerge, the reed and sedge take over. Amphibious *Persicaria*, its pink flowers appearing in July, is part of the emblem of the Cheshire Conservation Trust—you can find it near the main lake overflow. Two other plants of the marsh are an import from South America, with large spiny leaves, *Gunnera*, and great reed mace which many people confuse with the bulrush.

The return to the house from the lake's shallow valley is alongside a wall of old hand-made bricks. It has been discovered that inside the wall, flues have been built to conduct warm air through the brickwork. Fires would be lit and the heat would keep frost from damaging fruit trees trained against the wall in the es-palier fashion.

Capesthorne's Hall was altered by Blore in 1837 and Salvin in 1867 and today contains a great variety of treasures, from fine paintings to an unusual collection of antique and gim-micky walking sticks. The lake and Redesmere can be fished on a day ticket from the water bailiff, bream and carp being the particularly keenly hunted fish. There is some good coarse

fishing in the River Dane and the Macclesfield Canal.

A major landmark of the Cheshire Plain close to Capesthorne is the Nuffield Radio Astronomy Laboratory. Here radio telescopes bring new knowledge of the origins of the universe—the Mark I is a massive 250-foot steerable bowl facing skywards. A few yards from the telescope there is a planetarium giving regular shows of celestial events. The concourse building has a permanent exhibition of modern astronomy and, unusually, there is an arboretum.

North of Capesthorne on the A34 is the charming village of Nether Alderley clustered around the largely 14th-century church of St Mary. Nether Alderley is on lands once owned by the Stanley family—the same affluent land-owners with interests in Anglesey (see pages 46 and 47). The most prominent building of the village, seen from the main road, is the National Trust-owned watermill. Dating back to the mid 15th-century the mill, fed by water from Radnor Mere, once had two millstones (there is a worn one by the mill door) and was in operation until as recently as 1939. All the machinery is preserved and the mill is open to the public at certain times.

Macclesfield celebrates its continuing links with the silk industry (now largely displaced by companies producing modern textiles in the town) in an exhibition of the skills and technology used in working with this beautiful material at the town's museum. The museum also has a notable collection of Egyptian anti-quities and works by C F Tunnicliffe and Landseer in the art gallery.

Balancing the stately gardens of Capes-thorne on Macclesfield's east flank is the sharp rise to the peaks through the Macclesfield Forest. From Tegg's Nose Country Park on the forest's edge it is possible to walk across the Derbyshire border into the Peak District National Park, ending a half day's ramble at the Cat and Fiddle Inn. Set in lonely moorland at 1690 feet, this is one of the highest public houses in Britain.

Angling
Lamaload Reservoir: fly fishing for trout near Macclesfield. Daily tickets: R Newton, 5 Park Lane, Macclesfield *Tel: (0625) 24978* Water Authority: NWWA, New Town House, Buttermarket Street, Warrington *Tel: (0925) 53999* Macclesfield Canal: fair coarse fishing with good access. Daily tickets & Water Authority: as Lamaload Reservoir

Camping
Buxton: Dukes Drive Caravan Site ▶ *Tel: (0298) 2777* Simple 25-pitch site Open Mar–Oct, no bookings Whaley Bridge: Happy Vans Caravan Site ▶ *Tel: (061 483) 8888* Grassy 6-pitch site (no tents) 9m NE of Macclesfield off A6. Open all year, must book Jul–Aug

Golfing
Buxton & High Peak: *Tel: (0298) 3453* Scenic meadowland course. 18 holes, 5913yds, par 70, SSS68 Macclesfield: *Tel: (0625) 23227* Hilly heathland course, 11 holes, 6184yds, par 71, SSS69 Prestbury: *Tel: (0625) 48241* Undulating parkland course 2m N of Macclesfield, 18 holes, 6359yds, par 71, SSS71

Riding
Knutsford: Altrincham & District Riding Academy

(Capt N Milton), Bucklow Hill, near Knutsford *Tel: (0565) 830238*

General
Adlington: Adlington Hall. Tudor banqueting hall plus gardens, 4m E of Wilmslow off B5358 Open Apr–Sep Sun 2.30–6, plus Wed & Sat Jul–Aug *Tel: (0625) 829206* Buxton: Museum & Art Gallery: local history, minerals & ceramics, plus many water-colour paintings Open all year (ex Sun) *Tel: (0298) 4658* Holmes Chapel: Jodrell Bank: the famous radio telescope, plus working models & displays, 4m NE of Holmes Chapel off A535 Open mid-Mar–Oct daily 2–6, plus weekends only in winter *Tel: (047 77) 339* Macclesfield: Gawsworth Hall: interesting Tudor manor house, 4m SW of Macclesfield off A536 Open mid-Mar–Oct daily 2–6 *Tel: (026 03) 456* Macclesfield Museum & Art Gallery: Egyptian relics & silk displays Open all year Tue–Sat, plus Sun afternoons *Tel: (0625) 24067* Nether Alderley: Alderley Old Mill: 15th-century mill, 4m S of Wilmslow off A34 Open Apr–Oct Wed & Sun 2–5.30, plus daily (ex Mon) Jul–Sep

Slurring Rock Nature Trail

Metropolitan Borough of Calder, Information Centre, 1 Bridge Gate, Hebden Bridge, West Yorkshire, HX7 8JP

Tel: Hebden Bridge (042 284) 3831

On unclassified road off A6033 1¼ miles north of Hebden Bridge centre – signposted Hardcastle Crags

Map reference: SD997291

Approximately 2-mile trail along valley of Hebden Water, woodlands and rock escarpment – beautiful aspects compared to Switzerland by Swiss visitors

Facilities: Illustrated trail guide; car parks; close to National Trust Hardcastle Crags

---

Just as the tide of the industrial revolution brought the black satanic mills to Hebden Bridge, equally ferocious commercial forces have now closed their doors. Gone are the corduroy cloth mills whose clattering looms worked through the night until the Fifties. The mill-hands' sooty back-to-back houses are being cleaned and renovated. Even the Rochdale Canal, which used to be clogged with horse-drawn barges bringing coal into the town and taking cotton out, is today a haven of peace for the fisherman.

Hebden Bridge has left the mighty wheels of industry to the great conurbations of Yorkshire and Lancashire which flank the town on each side. It has become a sanctuary for those working in Leeds or Manchester, being a commutable distance away; and in recent years, a favourite spot with walkers. For the surrounding countryside is the wild, desolate moorland of the South Pennines, with a sprinkling of wooded valleys and tiny villages hewn out of solid sandstone and millstone grit. Those who love the thatched cottages of Sussex would probably not appreciate this area's wild beauty. It was this savage scenery which gave inspiration to the Brontë sisters – they lived just north of Hebden Bridge at Haworth.

There are over 130 walks in the South Pennines, all within a twenty mile radius of Hebden Bridge. One, Slurring Rock Nature Trail, explores the National Trust-owned woodland of Hardcastle Crags, although ramblers are free to find their own walks both here and in Crimsworth Dene.

The first leg of the Slurring Rock trail passes through the ancient Manor of Wadsworth, which was lorded by the Savile family from the Middle Ages. Unwisely, the first Lord Savile felled great stretches of woodland in the late 19th century, and the mixed deciduous and coniferous trees of today are comparatively young. They are inhabited by the rare and almost extinct red squirrel and by a variety of nesting birds in spring.

The Wadsworth estate was separated from Heptonstall by Hebden Water, a fast-flowing stream which attracts its own forms of plant and animal life. Dippers and wagtails are frequent visitors, and where the river cliff constantly trickles with water, moisture-loving plants such as herb Robert, wood sorrel and golden saxifrage have taken hold.

Here and there along the route are reminders of the industrial past: weirs, to summon the power to drive water wheels; the sites of once-active mills and the ruins of weavers' cottages. At the heart of Hebden Valley is the best-preserved water-driven cotton mill, Gibson Mill. Three-storeys high, with a group of workers' cottages nestling beneath it, it was built in 1800 and converted to steam power around sixty years later. By the turn of the century the machines were silent.

Features of the trail have local names which are a strange mixture of ancient and modern languages. Clearings in the woodlands are named 'royd' a mediaeval word, combined into many place-names. A low-lying meadow near the river is called *The Holme*, a Norse word meaning an island or low-lying land close to a lake or river. Stepping stones are 'hippins', and the trail itself is so-called because generations of children have been sliding or 'slurring' down the highest point of the walk, where the Lower Kinderscout Grits overlie the Sabden Shales and form an escarpment.

On one June day each year, the lush Holme and the green woods around it echo with the voices of another language. This is the site of the Annual Swiss Landsgemeinde, an event which draws all Swiss nationals living in England together. The spot was chosen since it resembles, in scenery, the place in Switzerland where the Republic was founded.

Before the industrial revolution, the inhabitants of these woodlands would have pursued work other than weaving. The trail skirts a small quarry where rock for repairing roads was cut; and the glades are scattered with charcoal hearths. They span generations of solitary burners, for felling took place only every twenty-five to thirty years. The valley floor supported farms. Hebden Hey Farm, now owned by Halifax's Scouts Association, would have bred sheep for wool, as the woollen industry was established here in the 13th century.

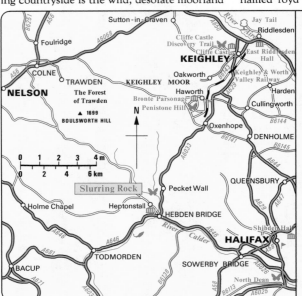

Cliffe Castle Discovery Trail
3 signposted walks through parkland, passing aviaries and conservatories. Start from Cliffe Castle Museum, Keighley
Open all year

Jay Tail Nature Trail
2m circular woodland walk. Start at Elam Wood Road, Riddlesden, near Keighley
Open all year

North Dean Nature Trail
2–5m parkland walk, featuring derelict railway and quarries. Start at Clay House, 3m S of Halifax off B6113
Open all year

Penistone Hill
Numerous trails within country park. Start 3m SW of Keighley at end of B6144
Open all year

Angling
River Calder: a Ribble tributary offering fair coarse fishing
Daily tickets: Northern Angling Association (G Wilson), 11 Guildford Avenue, Chorley
Tel: (025 72) 5905
Water Authority: NWWA, New Town House, Buttermarket Street, Warrington
Tel: (0925) 53999
Harold Park Lake: mixed fishing near Bradford
Daily tickets (in advance): Angling Stores Ltd, 938 Leeds Road, Bradford
Tel: (0274) 663767
Water Authority: YWA, West Riding House, 67 Albion Street, Leeds
Tel: (0532) 448201

Camping
Lothersdale: Springs Caravan Park ►►
Tel: (0535) 32533
Rural 30-pitch site 6m NE of Colne off A6068
Open Mar–Oct

Golfing
Halifax:
Tel: (0422) 244171
Scenic moorland course, 18 holes, 6034yds, par 70, SSS70
West Bradford:
Tel: (0274) 427671
Breezy parkland course, 18 holes, 5474yds, par 69, SSS67
West End (Halifax):
Tel: (0422) 53068
Moorland course, 18 holes, 6003yds, par 69, SSS69

General
Bradford: Bolling Hall: 15th-century house, now local history & furniture museum
Open all year daily 10–5
Tel: (0274) 23057
Industrial Museum: featuring transport & textiles
Open all year daily 10–5
Tel: (0274) 631756
Halifax: Shibden Hall: 15th-century building housing folk museum
Open all year (ex Feb–Sun only)
Tel: (0422) 52246
Haworth: Brontë Parsonage: home of the famous literary family
Open all year daily (ex Sun mornings & last three weeks of Dec)
Tel: (0535) 42323
Hebden Bridge: Heptonstall Grammar School Museum: 17th-century village school with original desks
Open all year, Sat & Sun only
Tel: (042 284) 3738
Keighley: Cliffe Castle: 19th-century mansion housing dolls & ceramics museum, plus grounds
Open all year daily 10–5
Tel: (0535) 64184
East Riddlesden Hall: 17th-century house with fine tithe barn
Open Apr–Oct (ex mon & Tue) 2–6; Jun–Aug 10.30–6.30

Some traditions have kept going throughout Hebden Bridge's history of change. It is renowned for its brass band and Morris dancing country and like most of the surrounding villages, a Pace Egg Play is held each year on Good Friday. The locals eat Dock Pudding each spring – a mixture of sweet dock (which grows profusely), young nettles, onions and oatmeal which is first boiled, then fried and served with bacon and potatoes.

There are almost as many golf courses in the North as there are towns, and the nearest to Hebden Bridge is the pleasant moorland course at Todmorden. Pony trekking over the wild countryside is gaining popularity and rock climbers find faces at Widdop and Heptonstall. Anglers are put in a quandary, for although the Rochdale Canal is well-stocked with coarse fish (especially large bream), the water is uncharacteristically clear for a canal, and the fish elusive.

Heptonstall, which overlooks Hebden Bridge is another historic village, perhaps best explored by following a walk described in a booklet published by the Calder Civic Trust. The Old Grammar School, which was founded in 1642, is a museum today, exhibiting relics of both the school and the village, and nearby are the ruins of the Church of St Thomas à Becket, which was begun round 1256. Like Mankinholes and Luddenden, Heptonstall was a well-known handloom weaving village, and the houses have the characteristic mullioned windows which let the maximum amount of light into the room and on to the looms.

Several miles to the north are the windswept

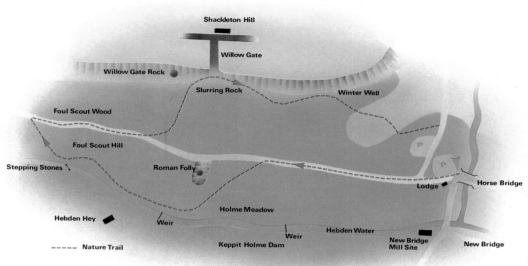

moors of Haworth – Brontë country. Their home, the Parsonage, retains their presence in a collection of relics, and not surprisingly, the steep village street is lined with gift shops, cafés and galleries. Nearby is the Keighley and Worth Valley Railway depot where monsters of the age of steam are housed. At weekends enthusiasts can take a ride along the standard-gauge line, or just admire the engines.

Just over the border into Lancashire is Towneley Hall – a 14th-century house set in 200 acres of parkland furnished with early English water colours, period furniture, ivories and 18th-century glass. The Hall holds various sporting activities throughout the summer and there is also a woodland trail.

For the more serious walker, there is the challenge of the 250-mile Pennine Way which stretches from Edale in Derbyshire to Kirk Yetholm on the Scottish border. There is also the New Calderdale Way, a fifty-mile circular route in the valley of the Calder River.

Reflections in the canal near Hebden Bridge

Reginald Farrer Trail

Yorkshire Dales National Park
Centre, Clapham,
North Yorkshire
Tel: Clapham (046 85) 419

Trail starts at National Park Centre in
village of Clapham on A65 between
Settle (6 miles) and Kendal (23 miles)

Map reference: SD745692

4–4½-mile trail illustrating social,
historical and geological impact on a
limestone landscape. National Park
Centre open Easter–early November
(mid-morning–late afternoon)

Facilities: Illustrated trail brochure; car
park; exhibition in Centre; (small
charge made for entry into Ingleborough
Estate grounds)

Nestling under the imposing bulk of the 2375-
foot-high peak of Ingleborough, is the tiny
Yorkshire Dales village of Clapham, clustered
around the waters of Clapham Beck outside the
gates of Ingleborough Hall. The hall was for
five generations the home of the Farrer family
who interpreted their responsibilities to tenants in a benevolent style, rebuilding the village and landscaping the Ingleborough grounds
as a recreational benefit for people from miles
around for over more than a hundred years.
The major work was the creation of a landscaped ornamental garden and artificial lake in
the deep valley carved by Clapham Beck's
passage through the soft limestone rock of the
Dales. Walks and carriage drives took visitors
up the valley to the natural attraction of Ingleborough Cave and these old roads and paths
form the basis for today's Reginald Farrer Trail,
designed by the Yorkshire Dales National Park
to commemorate both the family's most famous son and European Conservation Year
(1970).

Reginald Farrer was an extraordinarily
talented man. Successful as a painter and
novelist he was also a noted explorer and
botanist. For much of his life he explored Asia
and collected and identified several hundred
new plant species, many of which he brought
back to Ingleborough to enhance the shrub-
beries. Rhododendrons, of which he found
twenty-four new varieties, were a particular
favourite of his. Loving the east so well – he
became a practising Buddhist – it is fitting that
he died in Burma in 1920 but a tragedy that he
was only forty years old.

The commemorative trail sets out from the
National Park Centre in the village and follows
the line of the Clapdale carriage drive up the
valleys and into the lower slopes of Ingleborough peak. Clap Beck on the valley floor
is dammed to form the 700-yard lake to the
right of the track. The lake provides the village

with water and gave Clapham electric street
lights by hydro-electric power long before this
was commonplace. The first wood you reach
contains ornamental species such as red oak
(*Quercus borealis*), silver fir and the spiral
barked trunks of sweet chestnut. More dominant are somewhat displaced trees such as the
south of England's evergreen holm oak (*Quercus ilex*), Weymouth and Scots pines and yew.

The north tip of the lake, where the path
begins to rise, marks the line of the North
Craven geological fault where slabs of Ordovi-
cian rock are thrust through the limestone
cover of the Dales. Here the ground becomes
more acidic enabling Farrer to vary his garden
with some rhododendrons that prefer these
conditions. Another Farrer import is a patch of
himalayan bamboo. It is probable that neither
would survive if the valley were not sheltered
from cold winds blowing over the moor tops.

The path passes a curious stone grotto of the
kind many landscapers would design to provide
amusement and talking points to estate visitors
– this one is in a Moorish style. Around here
are coniferous plantations of Scots pine and
Sitka spruce among which you will see ash and
sycamore. The Ingleborough woods are managed like those of Felbrigg (p 32) in co-
operation with the Forestry Commission. In
another 200 yards or so is Ingleborough Cave.

Opened up by James and Oliver Farrer in
1837, the cave was once sealed off by stalag-
mites of water-deposited lime and contained a
considerable volume of water which was re-
leased to allow entry into the main cavern.
Guided tours are taken around the cave at
certain times which are displayed on a board at
the cave mouth. This is the lower end of a
mile-long underground water system of inter-
linked caverns and passages eroded out of the
hillside from the point at which Fell Beck
plunges 365 feet down the pot-hole of Gaping
Gill. This system, not yet fully explored by
pot-holers, is the source of Clapham Beck and
several other nearby springs which tap into the
mass of water held in this limestone hill. The
narrow Trow Gill, which the trail now enters,
is the previous path of the stream that has now
disappeared underground and sensible walkers
will be wearing stout shoes to scramble up the
ravine. Mosses and liverworts grow in the wet
sheltered habitats of the limestone rock piles
and there is a considerable undergrowth of
nettles in parts thriving on the minerals of
freshly broken, phosphate-rich rock.

Trow Gill is the trail's furthest point – the
easier return is by the same path back to
Clapham. Only slightly longer and more
energetic is to skirt the foot of the Clapham
Bottom's heath pasture to the east and join a

good section of an old pack-horse and drovers' road called Long Lane. If you are a more ambitious walker you will have picked up the leaflets at the park centre that will guide you on to Gaping Gill and, perhaps the summit of Ingleborough itself.

Long Lane is at about 900 feet high on the valley side and offers excellent views down to the mouth of the valley and, on fine days, to the steep rise of the Forest of Bowland. The trail passes from rough sheep pasture to border tree plantation areas before joining another ancient right of way called Thwaite Lane which leads back to Clapham through a couple of unusual tunnels taking the travellers under the grounds of Ingleborough Hall. Clapham church at the path's end was substantially rebuilt by the Farrer family and contains memorials to most of Reginald's forebears, although, as a Buddhist, he has no stone here – the grounds he helped to create are his best tribute.

Clapham is close to the National Park's western boundary. At the heart of the park is the beautiful setting of Malham, its Tarn and the grandeur of Malham Cove where 300-foot cliffs form a bowl in which the source of the River Aire lies. Tarn House, its drive forming part of the 250-mile Pennine Way long-distance footpath, is where Charles Kingsley wrote part of *The Water Babies*. It is now a teaching centre of the Field Studies Council which has designed a nature trail around the lake's north and east shores on National Trust land. Malham village hosts an annual autumn sheep sale that has been in existence for over 200 years and if you still have your walking boots on you will be welcome in the hikers' bar of the Buck Inn.

Campers fare very well within the National Park. There are sites in picturesque settings at Skipton, Stainforth, Threshfield and, just outside the park, High Bentham. Skipton is an attractive Airedale town with an 11th-century castle which is still partially lived-in. It is open to view. The town is on the Leeds–Liverpool Canal, the last remaining navigable trans-Pennine waterway and it was at Skipton that the canal company held its inaugural meeting in 1770. Canal trips can be taken to view some of the sturdy wharfside architecture and gardens of the town.

At Grassington, Malham, Aysgarth and Leyburn are National Park Centres where you will find information on a host of other walking trails and outdoor pursuits within the Yorkshire Dales.

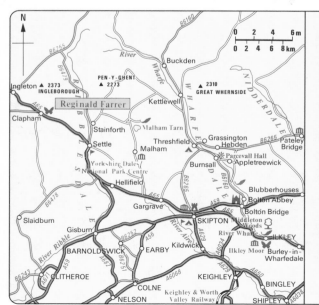

Ilkley Moor Nature Trail
2m circular moorland route rich in natural history. Start at paddling pool, Wells Road, Ilkley Moor
Open all year

Malham Tarn Nature Trail
1½m lakeside walk rich in birds and geology. Start from Warden's house, Malham Tarn Field Centre, Malham Moor (6m E of Settle)
Open all year

Middleton Woods
3½m trail through oaks and bluebell fields. Start at Curly Hill, 1½m N of Ilkley off A65
Open all year

River Wharfe Nature Walks
3½m riverside trail featuring midway stepping stones. Start at Ilkley New Bridge, ½m N of Ilkley off A65
Open all year

Angling
Greenfield Lake: fly fishing for trout, near Skipton
Daily tickets: Buck Inn, Buckden
Water Authority: as River Wharfe
River Wharfe: mainly fly-only trout fishing with abundant access
Daily tickets (in advance):
Devonshire Hotel, Grassington
Tel: (0756) 752525 or Cree's Pet Stores, 23 Leeds Road, Ilkley
Tel: (0943) 609594
Water Authority: YWA, West Riding House, 67 Albion Street, Leeds
Tel: (0532) 448201

Camping
Skipton: Overdale Trailer Park ▶▶
Tel: (0756) 3480
Mainly level 20-pitch site (no tents)
Open all year, must book
Threshfield: Long Ashes Caravan Park ▶▶▶
Tel: (0756) 752261
Level 120-pitch site (no tents) 1½m W of Grassington off B6265
Open mid-Mar–Oct, must book Jul–Aug

Golfing
Settle: scenic parkland course, 9 holes, 4590yds, par 64, SSS64
Skipton:
Tel: (0756) 3257

Tough heathland course, 12 holes, 5830yds, par 69, SSS68

General
Burnsall: Parcevall Hall Gardens: Elizebethan manor's lovely grounds, 8m NE of Skipton off B6160
Open Easter–Sep
Tel: (075 672) 214
Ilkley: Manor House: 16th-century mansion built on site of Roman fort
Open daily 10–5
Tel: (0943) 600066
Malham: Yorkshire Dales National Park Centre: permanent displays, books & maps
Open Apr–Sep daily
Tel: (072 93) 363
Pateley Bridge: Niderdale Museum: local costume, farming & domestic displays, 12m E of Grassington off B6265
Open Easter–Sep daily 2–5, plus Sun only in winter
Tel: (0423) 711225
Skipton: Craven Museum: mining, folk & archaeological exhibits
Open all year (ex Tue & Sun mornings)
Tel: (0756) 4079
Skipton Castle: 12th–14th-century fortress with huge gateway
Open all year daily (ex Sun mornings)
Tel: (0756) 2442

Smithy Beck and Dodd Wood Trails

Forestry Commission, 1a
Helvellyn Street, Keswick,
Cumbria
Tel: Keswick (0596) 73195

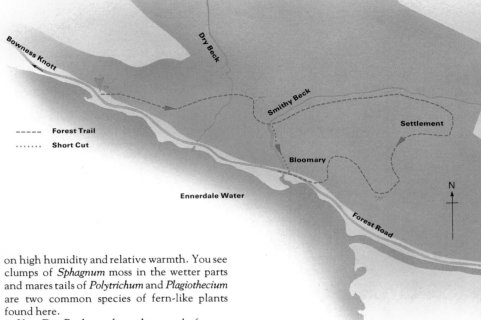

----- Forest Trail

.... Short Cut

Bowness Knott

Dry Beck

Smithy Beck

Settlement

Bloomary

Ennerdale Water

Forest Road

N

Smithy Beck Forest Trail
At end of unclassified road through
hamlet of Croasdale 2 miles north east
of Ennerdale Bridge at Bowness Knott
car park

Map reference: NY108155 (Bowness
Knott car park)

Approx 2½-mile trail through Ennerdale
Forest with spectacular lakeland views.
Some steep sections

Dodd Wood Forest Trail
On A591 2½ miles south of
Bassenthwaite village, 3½ miles north of
Keswick

Map reference: NY235282

1½-mile trail through woods on the
foreslopes of Skiddaw with footpath
access to the summit if feeling
energetic. Some steep sections – good
shoes essential

Facilities: Illustrated trail guides: car
parks

The Lake District is a compact 900-square mile
National Park of stunning beauty which not
only includes breathtaking lake views – it also
has some of the highest mountains in England.
There are almost sixty stretches of stillwater
within the Park's bounds, nestling among
peaks like the monarch Scafell Pike (3210ft),
the rounded flanks of Helvellyn, Skiddaw and
Great Gable. The major lakes divide naturally
into those of the southern Lake District such as
Windermere and Coniston, most popular for
their ready access from the M6, and the more
northern lakes towards the coast and around
the major centre of Keswick. It is to Ennerdale
and Bassenthwaite in this northern group, a
little out of the way of the heavy crowds, that
the walker can find two lake, forest and fell
trails which show off both the scenic beauty
and the Lakes' varied wildlife.

Smithy Beck Forest Trail combines an enjoyable walk along the Ennerdale Water shore
with a climb through a varied forest with
breaks in the trees that reveal superb views of
the high fells surrounding this most westerly of
the major lakes. Climbing through woods of
Japanese larch and Scots pine you will also see
some of the more natural trees of the Lakes –
the sessile oak, mountain ash, birch and
hawthorn. Under the dense cover of trees, the
light level is low and the predominant plants
are simple mosses and liverworts which thrive

on high humidity and relative warmth. You see
clumps of *Sphagnum* moss in the wetter parts
and mares tails of *Polytrichum* and *Plagiothecium*
are two common species of fern-like plants
found here.

If at Dry Beck you hear the sound of water
and yet can see little moisture, you will under-
stand its name. Here and there the water
emerges but it actually trickles down through
rock clefts for most of its journey to the lake.
There is a good place here for a natural break in

the trees which is not only a fire safeguard but
it is also a visual relief from the dense conifers.
Soon you come to Smithy Beck itself and a
superb vantage point overlooking the stream
valley, Ennerdale Water and, beyond, the fell

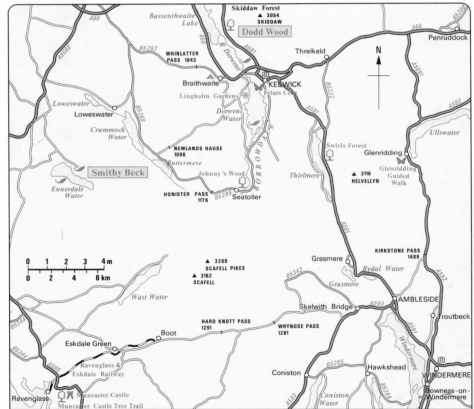

Friars Crag
1½m National Trust trail. Start
from car park, northern end of
Keswick off A591
Open all year

Glenridding Guided Walk
2m trail through fells surrounding
Lake Ullswater. Start from
Beckside car park, Glenridding,
9m SE of Keswick off A592
Open mid-Apr–mid-Sep, Sun
only, plus Wed mid-Jul–Aug

Johnny's Wood Nature Trail
2m woodland walk with
marvellous 927ft viewpoint. Start
from Seatoller car park, Seatoller,
7m SW of Keswick off B5289
Open all year

Muncaster Castle Tree Trail
1½m walk amongst numerous
shrubs and trees. Start at
Muncaster Castle gate, 1m E of
Ravenglass off A595
Open Apr–Sep daily 12–5

Swirls Forest Trail
1m gradual climb through mixed
woodland. Start from car park,
7m SE of Keswick off A591 by
Thirlmere
Open all year

Derwent Fells

tops of Iron Crag topping 2000ft and Lank Rigg (1775ft).

The beck is named after the small iron smelting works once to be found at the mouth of the stream. The smithy forge would have been heated by charcoal made locally in the traditional turf-covered firing hearths otherwise known as pitsteads.

The path continues by crossing the beck and climbing higher above the older trees to the damp moorland under Gale Fell. The plants here reflect the poor nutritive value of the rain-leached soil – typical examples are purple moor grass, bog asphodel, and deer grass. At the path's furthest point from the car park are the remains of a medieval settlement. There is another viewpoint on the way back to the lake shore which enables you to see over Ennerdale and, to the west, up the valley towards Pillar (2927ft) and the stack of Pillar Rock.

The forest trail and walks of Dodd Wood are through woods on the foreslopes of Skiddaw by the Derwent's inflow into Bassenthwaite Lake ('thwaite', a common suffix in the Lakes, is from the Norse for a clearing in woodlands). Dodd has been a man-made woodland since the late 18th century, when Thomas Story of the Mirehouse estate first planted conifers such as the silver fir and European larch. Some of these trees remain at the foot of the Skill Beck valley through which the trail climbs. Water from the beck was dammed in the mill pond which was used to power wood-cutting machinery.

Douglas firs here, planted in about 1930 have grown to as high as one hundred feet in the favourable conditions of the lower wood. Further up the track you will see the same aged trees some forty feet lower in stature due to the exposure on higher slopes. The tall trees are used as seed-bearing stock to improve trees for the future. The natural rock of the area, exposed at various points along the path is the Skiddaw slate widely quarried and used for road-making.

When the older trees are felled at about forty-five years of age, they have been replaced by the ubiquitous Sitka spruce which withstands the poor conditions on high ground a lot better. Japanese larch is mixed in to the new trees at random to provide a little visual contrast with its russet twigs – it is an unusual deciduous conifer.

Animals of these woods are not present in large numbers – but most of them are not at all common and will be a delight if you do actually see them. Rarest of all is the rapid-climbing pine marten and the red squirrel is still here in depleted numbers. Roe deer graze on young tree shoots and they are excluded from young woodlands wherever it is possible. Badgers and

foxes will rarely be seen, but they are here. Overhead birds of prey are prominent – you may be lucky enough to see the buzzard plummet for small mammals or birds. The kestrel can take small birds while on the wing. Nocturnal hunters are the tawny owls which can occasionally be seen by day.

At the trail's furthest point from the main road it meets the Skill Beck where you may like to rest and observe the life of the wetter regions of the stream banks. Mosses and liverworts such as *Sphagnum* and *Lunularia* are in water-splashed pockets, and rushes abound. Along the beck, some non-commercial trees such as rowan and oak have been left to vary the wildlife habitats of the valley. You walk back along a track on the opposite side of the valley.

Bassenthwaite Lake below Dodd Wood is owned by the Lake District Special Planning Board as a leisure amenity. It has good stocks of trout, perch and pike and there is a salmon run. It can be fished with locally available permits. On nearby Derwentwater, and the short stretch of the River Derwent between these lakes, Keswick Anglers' Association control some fishing rights and visitors can obtain

tickets. If you are a small boat sailor you can sail on both lakes but no powered craft are allowed on Bassenthwaite. Fishing Ennerdale water is more tightly controlled – the Calder Angling Association have a limited number of permits.

The Lake District is a paradise for lovers of the great outdoors. Campsites abound in both the north and south of the area – handy for the two trails are sites at Bassenthwaite, Braithwaite, Troutbeck and Cockermouth. To avoid the almost inevitable traffic jams at holiday peaks you can hire a bicycle from centres at Cockermouth and Keswick.

Angling
Bassenthwaite: boat fishing for perch, pike & trout
Daily tickets: Bassenthwaite Post Office
Water Authority: as River Derwent
River Derwent: good trout fishing plus pike & perch
Daily tickets (in advance): Egremont Estate Co (riparian owner), The Castle, Cockermouth
Tel: (0900) 823472
or Temple's, 9 Station Street, Keswick
Tel: (0596) 72569
Water Authority: NWWA, New Town House, Buttermarket Street, Warrington
Tel: (0925) 53999
Derwent Water: good for perch & trout plus some salmon
Daily tickets & Water Authority: as River Derwent
Ennerdale Water: good for trout May–Jul
Daily tickets: Wath Brow Post Office, Cleator Moor
Water Authority: as River Derwent

Camping
Braithwaite: Scotgate Caravan Site ▶
Tel: (059 682) 343
Rural 135-pitch site (15 caravans)
Open Mar–Oct, no bookings
Cockermouth: Violet Bank Caravan Site ▶▶▶
Tel: (0900) 822169
Well-kept 40-pitch site
Open Apr–Oct, no bookings

Golfing
Cockermouth:
Tel: (059 681) 223

Scenic fell course 4m E of Cockermouth off A66, 18 holes, 5457yds, par 69, SSS67
Seascale:
Tel: (094 02) 202
Tough links course, 18 holes, 6307yds, par 71, SSS70
Workington:
Tel: (0900) 3460
Undulating meadowland course, 18 holes, 6250yds, par 71, SSS70

General
Cockermouth: Wordsworth House: the poet's birthplace, with original furnishings
Open Apr–Oct daily (ex Thu)
Keswick: Castlerigg Stone Circle: prehistoric stones 1m W of town
Accessible at all times
Fitz Park Museum & Art Gallery: rare Walpole & Southey relics
Open Apr–Oct daily (ex Sun)
Tel: (0596) 73263
Lingholm: formal shrub gardens & woodland walk, 2½m W of Keswick off A66
Open Apr–Oct daily 10–5 (ex Sun)
Tel: (0596) 72003
Ravenglass: Ravenglass and Eskdale Railway: 15in-gauge 7m track through beautiful scenery
Open 30 Mar–2 Nov daily 7.45–6.40
Whitehaven: Whitehaven Museum & Art Gallery: local history, mining, shipbuilding & pottery
Open all year (ex Sun)
Tel: (0946) 3111 ext 289

Forest Trail
Carlisle
A591
Keswick
N
Skill Beck
Longside Wood
Tarmac Road
Dodd Wood
Summit

May Beck Trail

North York Moors National Park,
The Old Vicarage, Bondgate,
Helmsley, YO6 5BP
Tel: Helmsley (0439) 70657

1¾ miles off B1416 on unclassified road
between Ruswarp and junction with
A171

Map reference: NZ892024

4-mile trail around a moor farm, open
moorland and a conifer
plantation—shows the hard life of the
moor farmer and the harmony of
forestry, game and farming interests

Facilities: Trail booklet from National
Park and tourist information offices; car
park

Extending from the Cleveland and Hambledon Hills for 600 square miles to the high cliffs
of Yorkshire's northern coast, the North York
Moors National Park consists in the main of
heather-clad moorland. It can be a bleak environment, but for centuries man has struggled
to raise animals here and reclaim land for
arable use. May Beck Trail which climbs on to
Fylingdales Moor, better known for the 40-
foot diameter golf balls of the missile early
warning system, explores the hard life of farming the moor fringes.

May Beck Farm lies in a fold of the sombre

Fylingdales Moor above the thinly wooded
valley of May Beck itself. The farmhouse is of a
traditional long-house design with the farmer's
cottage attached to, and in line with, the main
animal buildings and cornstore. It is a typical
moorland sheep farm on which there are about
300 predominantly pure-bred Swaledale sheep,
and a herd of cross-bred cattle (Galloway cows
breeding Hereford and Charolais crosses) producing beef calves for sale. The trail starts at a
Forestry Commission car park half a mile past
the farm at the point where the road crosses
May Beck.

Much of the farmer's battle is to provide
good grass for the animals. On the first part of
the walk are grazing enclosures on which poor
management of the past has allowed a natural
bracken cover to re-establish itself. Today's
tenant on the farm is fighting back the bracken
to improve the grazing quality. Some of the
land to the right of the road was reclaimed from
the moor as recently as 1977 by burning off
heather cover, drainage of wet areas, and liber-
al application of lime to counteract the natural
acidity, fertilisers and then grass seed. A healthy sward is now established here—but this is a
costly means of gaining land.

Some fields are used to grow hay as winter
feed for the animals. The hay is rotated with
other crops such as barley and turnips (also
animal feedstuffs) so that the ground remains
both fertile and weed-free. On May Beck
Farm, hay is stored for winter in a silage
clamp—natural fermentation and the weight of
the pile turns the grass into a brown and very
odorous, but nutritious, cake. The farmer has
bee hives in this lower pasture area—the bees
harvest the heather's nectar producing a honey
with a distinctive flavour.

From these lower pastures, the trail climbs
on to Shooting House Rigg (ridge) along which
a former pack horse and rough coaching road
once ran. Called Abbey Road, it once con-
nected Whitby with the regional capital of
York. On this high moorland of heather and
poor grass, farmers can exercise the right of
common grazing for their sheep. Inevitably the
sheep mingle with those of other flocks and so
a means of identification has to be used. This is
a combination of cuts in the ear, paint marks,
and horn brands. May Beck's distinctive
Swaledale sheep (both ewes and rams are
horned) have the left ear tip removed (stoud),
a red paint splash on the right shoulder and the
initials JS branded on the right horn. A crown
brand is a breed registration mark and the
number burned on the opposite horn indicates
the year the sheep was born.

While some game interests believe that
sheep and gamebirds do not live a complemen-
tary existence, on this moor there is co-
operation between the grouse breeders and the
farmers. Strips of heather are regularly burnt to
encourage new growth to feed both birds and
sheep. The attractive red grouse is the bird
reared on Fylingdales and shooting occurs between August 12th and December 10th.

The woods you see before you in the valley
of the Blea Hill Beck were planted around 1968
and are part of a whole new forest of 1400
acres. The trees are mainly lodgepole pine and

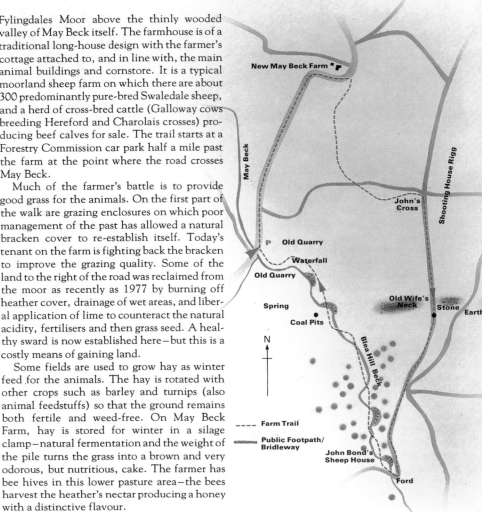

New May Beck Farm

May Beck

Shooting House Rigg

John's Cross

P Old Quarry

Waterfall

Old Quarry

Spring

Old Wife's Neck

Stone

Earthv

Coal Pits

N

Blea Hill Beck

- - - - Farm Trail

—— Public Footpath/
Bridleway

John Bond's
Sheep House

Ford

Sitka spruce, which are able to give a much
quicker economic return than broad-leaved
species, especially on the poor-draining and
deficient soils of the moor. Trees are not such
an incongruous crop here as you would im-
agine. During man's prehistoric period, the
whole of North Yorkshire is known to have
been covered with light forest. Oak, alder,
lime, willow, yew and pine pollens have all
been found in subsoil sections. Much of the
cover disappeared in the Bronze Age, when
mass clearance by fire began. Subsequent over-
grazing of the heathland has further deterior-
ated its quality.

The trail returns to the car park down the
valley of Blea Hill Beck which contains several
coalpits dug for fuel to fire the process of
alum-making in nearby Ravenscar. On wetter
parts of the path you may find bog myrtle,
which is used as a herb for flavouring a locally
made brew called gale beer. Just before the car
park is regained, the beck tumbles over a series
of delightful water falls to join May Beck and
the march of the new, young conifers gives way
to the older-established woodlands which follow the beck down through Falling Foss.

May Beck's trail does not only show the
struggles and rewards of moorland farming—it
deliberately illustrates the growing problems of
maintaining leisure amenity in areas where the
farming and forestry interests exist with those

Angling
River Esk: best
salmon fishing in N
Yorks
Daily tickets: F
Farrow, 11 Dale End,
Danby, Whitby or E
Wilson, 5
Haggersgate, Whitby
Tel: (0947) 3855
Water Authority:
YWA, West Riding
House, 67 Albion
Street, Leeds
Tel: (0532) 448201
Whitby: sand fishing
for bass, dab,
flounder & whiting.
Plus dogfish,
haddock & ray by
boat
Tackle shop: see
River Esk

Camping
Ugthorpe: Burnt
House Caravan
Park ►►►
Tel: (0947) 840448
86-pitch moorland
site (no tents)
Open Mar–Oct,
must book Jul–Aug
Whitby: Grouse Hill
Caravan Park ►►►
300-pitch moorland
site 8m S of Whitby
off A171
Open Apr–Oct, must
book Jul–Aug

Golfing
Whitby:
Tel: (0947) 2768

Breezy links course,
18 holes, 5980yds,
par 69, SSS67

General
Guisborough:
Guisborough Priory:
fine 14th-century
church remains
Accessible all year
Hutton-le-Hole:
Ryedale Folk
Museum: local
history & crafts, 7m
NW of Pickering
Open Easter–Sep
daily 2–5.30 (from 11
July–Aug)
Tel: (075 15) 367
Pickering: North
Yorkshire Moors
Railway (Moorsrail):
18m track, loco shed,
gift shop
Open Easter–early
Nov
Tel: (0751)
72508/73535
Pickering Castle:
12th-century
stronghold
Open all year
Whitby: Whitby
Abbey: extensive
remains of 13th-
century church
Open all year
Whitby Museum:
specialising in local
history, with Pannett
Art Gallery next door
Open May–Sep daily
9.30–5.30 (Sun 2–5)
Tel: (0947) 2908

of the game breeder. The North York Moors National Park hopes that visitors, by their interest and responsible behaviour in keeping to paths and observing the fire precautions, will prove that leisure uses can also exist in harmony with this cropping of the land.

May Beck, a world away in spirit, is only six miles from the coastal resort and fishing port of Whitby, clinging to the steep sides of the Esk estuary. The town's unusual blend of sedate turn-of-the-century boarding houses and hotels, brash seafront amusements and a quaint, old town make it an attractive touring centre for the whole of this high-cliffed coast. It is a thriving boat angling centre, drawing anglers from all over the north of England for stirring tussles with big ling, cod and conger. High above the old town, a long climb up interminable steps, is the 13th-century abbey on a site of a 7th-century monastery founded by St Hilda. Captain Cook made his first circumnavigation of the world in a Whitby-built ship and he stayed at No. 16 Grape Lane as a young apprentice.

Campers are well provided for along this coast – on Fylingdales Moor itself is the Grouse Hill Caravan Park and to the west of the town is the moor-edge Burnt House site, Ugthorpe.

To the south of Whitby, over the high tops of Goathland and Lockton moors by the A169 is the little town of Pickering. Rather than take the road, why not discover a hidden valley by the beautiful Moorsrail? Running a combination of diesel and steam trains over former British Rail track through Newtondale, the North Yorkshire Moors Railway travels between Grosmont in the Esk Valley (connections with British Rail) and Pickering eighteen miles away. Much of this route was pioneered by George Stephenson in 1836.

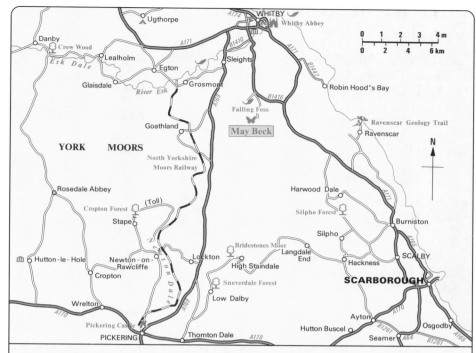

Bridestones Moor Nature Walk
1½m trail through woodland and crags. Start from High Staindale car park, 12m S of Whitby, 3m off A169
Open all year

Cropton Forest Walks
Several trails 1–4½m starting in forest drive 7m N of Pickering
Open all year

Crow Wood Trail
¼m signposted woodland walk. Start from Danby Lodge car park, Danby
Open all year

Falling Foss Nature Trail
3m riverside walk through mixed woodland. Start off B1416 4m S of Whitby
Open all year

Ravenscar Geology Trail
3m coastal walk of geological interest. Start from Falcon Inn, Ravenscar, Whitby
Open all year

Silpho (Langdale) Forest Trail
1¾m and 3m forest trails 7m NW of Scarborough via A171 and unclassified road N of Scalby
Open all year

Sneverdale Forest Trail
2½m woodland walk featuring sycamore and Douglas Fir. Start from car park, midway between Low Dalby and Hackness
Open all year

Whitby Abbey

Sutton Bank Trail

Yorkshire Naturalists' Trust, 20
Castlegate, York, YO1 1RP
Tel: York (0904) 59570

At Cooper Cross car park on A170
between Thirsk (5½ miles) and Helmsley
(6 miles)

Map reference: SE515830

2-mile trail down and around limestone
cliffs and woodland Nature Reserve –
some steep scrambling, so wear sturdy
shoes

Facilities: Illustrated trail brochure from
Trust, tourist and National Park offices;
car park; white horse (1857) to view

A few miles out of Thirsk, the main North
Yorkshire east–west road sweeps dramatically
upward by 500 feet within about half a mile in a
zig-zag course over the limestone escarpment of
Sutton Bank and into the Hambleton Hills.
Tumuli, prehistoric dyke earthworks and,
nearby, an ancient ridgway drovers' road makes
this a site of considerable historic interest. It is
also, in part, a Nature Reserve administered by
the Yorkshire Naturalists' Trust around which
a nature trail of about two miles loops.

Starting at the Sutton Bank summit car park
(Cooper Cross, an AA viewpoint) the trail
traverses the face of the bank for half a mile,
dropping about 400 feet down to the Garbutt
Wood Reserve. The first part of the trail,
following the way-marked Moors Path gives
superb views of the York plain and the Vale of
Mowbray. To your left is the limestone crag of
Roulston Scar with its cave, named the Devil's
Parlour, and, below, the unusual Gormire Lake
held in a fold of the hill amid a cluster of trees.
The cliffs not only provide the ideal upcurrents
of air to be utilised by the Yorkshire Gliding
Club from their bank-top field but you will see

kestrels hovering in these ideal conditions too.

Garbutt Wood, which you enter past a
boundary wall that is partly covered with mosses and herb Robert, is predominantly broad-
leaved hardwood including oak and ash scattered among birch. There are still some hazel
clumps remaining from the days when this
wood was coppiced – hazel was a major commodity used in weaving, besom-making,
fences and as firewood. The wood's animal
population includes badgers (you may be lucky
enough to spot the tracks in the softer earth of
their tracks), roe deer, fox and grey squirrel. At
times the glades echo to the drumming of the
greater spotted woodpecker in its quest for
insects, grubs or the less prominent note of its
cousin, the green woodpecker.

Within the wood's clearings are the typical
plants of a lime-filled sub-soil such as brackens
but you will also see small carpets of bluebells,
red campions and wild foxgloves. There are
some patches of more acid soil locally – principally on the higher parts of the path where

there is a foundation of calcareous grit. Here
the typical, mountain undergrowth of heather
and bilberry contrasts with the more varied
flora of the limestone areas.

The trail's highest point is under the slowly
eroding heights of Whitestone Cliff on which
a substantial landslide was once witnessed by
Charles Wesley while preaching in the hamlet
of Sutton. The rough and tumble of broken
rocks at the cliff's foot provides new opportunities for plant life to establish itself.
Lichens, mosses and liverworts are profuse.

Angling
River Rye: fly fishing
for trout with fair
access
Daily tickets:
Hawnby Hotel,
Hawnby
Tel: (043 96) 202
or D Grice,
Oswaldkirk Road,
Nunnington
Tel: (043 95) 247
Water Authority:
YWA, West Riding
House, 67 Albion
Street, Leeds
Tel: (0532) 448201

Camping
Harome: Foxholme
Caravan Park ▶▶▶
Tel: (043 92) 416
Level 30-pitch site
(no tents) 2m E of
Helmsley off A170
Open Easter–Oct, no
bookings
Thirsk: Trax
Campsite ▶▶
Mainly level 60-pitch
site
Open mid-May–mid-
Sep (ex May 30 & 31,
Aug 1 & 2, Sep 6), no
bookings

Golfing
Thirsk &

Northallerton:
Tel: (0845) 22170
Scenic moorland
course, 9 holes,
5379yds, par 65,
SSS66

General
Bedale: Bedale Hall:
Georgian house with
ballroom & museum.
Open May–Sep Tue
10–4, or by
appointment
Tel: (067 72) 3131
Coxwold: Shandy
Hall: mediaeval
house associated
with the author
Laurence Sterne, 8m
SE of Thirsk
Open Jun–Sep Wed
2–6, or by
appointment
Tel: (034 76) 465
Helmsley: Helmsley
Castle: remains of
12th/13th-century
stronghold
Open all year
Rievaulx: Rievaulx
Abbey: well-
preserved 12th-
century Cistercian
abbey, 3m NW of
Helmsley off B1257
Open all year

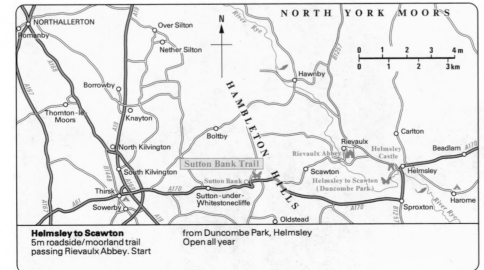

Helmsley to Scawton
5m roadside/moorland trail
passing Rievaulx Abbey. Start

from Duncombe Park, Helmsley
Open all year

Central &
South Scotland

5

Hopetoun House Nature Trail

Hopetoun House Preservation Trust, Estates Office, South Queensferry, West Lothian, EH30 9SL
Tel: (031–331 1546/1348/2451

On unclassified road 1 mile north of A904 2 miles west of Forth Road Bridge approach roundabout

Map reference: NT089790

2-mile trail in wooded and estuary shore grounds of 18th-century mansion – fallow deer and rare black St Kilda sheep

Facilities: Illustrated trail brochure; free park ranger guide service; house to tour (William Bruce and Adam family); wildlife exhibition; museum; picnic areas; restaurant/gift shop

Set like a precious stone in acres of parkland on the shores of the Firth of Forth, is the exquisite symmetry of Hopetoun House. Architecturally, it is one of the finest Adam mansions in Britain. Designed in 1699 by Sir William Bruce (the architect of Holyrood Palace Edinburgh), it was enlarged twenty-two years later by William Adam with the help of his two brilliant sons, John and Robert.

It was to be William Adam's last commission, for he died without seeing Hopetoun completed; but it was also his most outstanding, and it is this house that is represented on his tomb in Greyfriars churchyard.

Hopetoun has been the ancestral home of the Hope family since the first brick was laid, although in 1974 they formed a preservation trust to own the house and its valuable contents, and now live there as tenants. The interior is rich indeed, with walls lined in yellow silk brocade, gilded tables and priceless collections of books, china and costumes.

Most treasured of all is a stunning gallery of oil paintings by great masters such as Canaletto, Vandyke, Rubens and Titian. It was the 4th Earl of Hopetoun who bought most of the important canvases of the collection during his travels, in Genoa and London. Years later his direct descendant, the 7th Earl was created 1st Marquess of Linlithgow, the title which is used today.

Through the windows of the house are views of the Firth of Forth, spanned by a cantilevered railway bridge and a 2000-yard-long suspension road bridge. Immediately outside are straight, broad drives, sweeps of immaculate lawns and avenues of trees.

To the west of the house is yet another reason for spending a day at Hopetoun. A two-mile nature trail discovers another facet of this beautiful estate where creatures ranging from the majestic peacock to a humble wood-ant and myriads of other insects may be seen.

Visitors are invited to walk the trail in the company of one of the estate's rangers, a guided tour available from 1–6pm which is included in the admission price to the grounds. Many will prefer to take their time and spend longer than the estimated two to two-and-a-half hours.

Much of the trail skirts North Deer Park, twenty-five acres of rough grassland studded with beech, lime and oak trees. A sizeable herd of Britain's largest wild animal, the red deer, grazes here. Unlike these be-antlered bucks, the fallow deer of the south park are not natives of the country. They were probably brought across from Asia Minor by the Romans for hunting and to decorate their estates.

A wide variety of tree species gives a constantly changing pattern of shapes, fruits and flowers throughout the year – and a riot of colour in the autumn. Sugar maples from North America produce rich red leaves normally, which become pink-red in spring on shoots grafted onto sycamore stocks. There are several of these bizarre hybrid trees in the park, with the upper leaves different from the ones growing below. Aptly-named snowberry has dainty pink flowers which are followed by round milk-white berries, and in May the mighty horse chestnuts are aglow with candles of white or pink blossom. At least one Hopetoun yew is over 400 years old, and although like most coniferous varieties, it never changes its cloak of bottle green, it does produce a bright scarlet seed collar.

Hopetoun estate stretches to the shores of the Firth of Forth and from one point along the

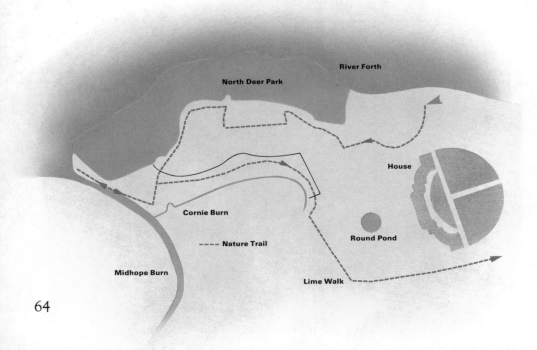

North Deer Park

River Forth

House

Cornie Burn

- - - Nature Trail

Round Pond

Midhope Burn

Lime Walk

trail there is a good view of the bridges and Fife and the Clackmannan coast and hills beyond. Super tankers penetrate the Firth as far as the manmade island, Hound Point oil terminal, to load crude oil from the offshore Forties field. The shore is a poor mixture of saltmarsh, sand, rocks and mudflats and supports little life apart from sandhoppers and scuttling shore crabs. It is always populated by crowds of oyster-catchers, gulls, ducks and terns, and conse-quently strewn with the empty shells of cock-les, mussels and whelks where they have fed.

Draining into the Firth from the estate is Cornie Burn – geologically a meltwater chan-nel from the last Ice Age. Its fertile valley has been planted with trees and shrubs chosen for their colour and fragrance, among them flow-ering currant, *Prunus*, sweet briar, box and lilac, while below are foxgloves, autumn crocus, cowslips and wood forget-me-not.

Throughout the walk there are reminders that this is part of a garden in which the Hope family have played and relaxed for centuries. They brought with them a stone eagle from Craighall, Ceres, Fife, their former home, and rescued three cannon from the Napoleonic Wars. In the woods are eleven headstones in memory of the family's pet dogs. In common with other affluent landowners of the 18th

century, the Hopes had a fashionable ha-ha built. This retaining wall ensured an uninter-rupted view of the parkland, while keeping the deer and less welcome animals at bay.

The last section of the nature trail passes groups of pea- and guinea-fowl. The peacock is resplendent with his fan of turquoise tail feath-ers, while his harem have tails which are dull brown. Like the fallow deer, these birds were probably brought to Britain by the Romans for decoration, although they proved a tasty feast for royalty in the Middle Ages. Less common occupants of Hopetoun's grasslands are a flock of St Kilda sheep which have thick black coats and four horns.

Queensferry South has been the crossing point for the Firth of Forth since ancient times, when a ferry plied between Hawes Pier and Hawes Inn. This 17th-century hostelry was described by Scott in *The Antiquary* and by Robert Louis Stevenson in *Kidnapped*. Queen Margaret of Scotland gave her name to Queensferry as she was a frequent ferry pas-senger. While her husband fought at the Battle of Flodden, she kept vigil in a tiny turret of Linlithgow Palace.

Mary, Queen of Scots was born here in 1542 and the fine building also had associations with Prince Charles Edward, George V and Oliver

Cromwell. Now ruined, the palace is still nota-ble for its quadrangle, chapel and great hall. An ornate fountain, a wedding present from James V to Mary of Guise, is said to have run with wine.

The House of The Binns is the historic home of the Dalyells which was converted from a fortress to an elegant home. One colourful son was General Tam Dalyell who raised the Royal Scots Greys here in 1681. Even today, mem-bers of the Royal Scots Dragoon Guards (suc-cessors to the Royal Scots Greys) are admitted to the house free of charge if they are in uniform.

Because of industrial pollution, the Forth is a fruitless river to fish, although experts have bagged salmon. Likewise its tributaries are dis-appointing in their lower reaches, although trout abound in the Almond at the Almondell and Calderwood Country Park. Here, 220 acres of woodland, rich in plant and wildlife provide a country playground for the industrial towns nearby. Even the rare and persecuted otter can be seen, most frequently at twilight.

Golfing enthusiasts are spoilt with a pletho-ra of courses around Edinburgh. On Hope-toun's side are Royal Burgess and Bruntisfield Links, which overlook the Forth, and Turn-house and Ratho Park.

Angling
River Almond: some chances of trout for visitors
Free fishing from Whitburn to Mid Calder (alongside A705)
Water of Leith: Edinburgh's now-good trout stream
Free tickets (in advance): Lothian Regional Council, Administration Dept, George IV Bridge, Edinburgh
Tel: 031-229 9292

Camping
Edinburgh: Morton Hall Caravan Park ▶▶▶▶
Tel: 031-664 1533
Large 250-pitch site
Open mid-Mar–Oct, must book Jul–Aug

Golfing
Dunfermline:
Tel: (0383) 23534
Pleasant parkland course, 18 holes, 6134yds, par 71, SSS69
Pitreavie:
Tel: (0383) 22591
Breezy upland course 2m SE of Dunfermline off B916, 18 holes, 6086yds, par 70, SSS69
Royal Burgess (Edinburgh):
Tel: 031-336 2075
Historic parkland course, 18 holes, 6604yds, par 71, SSS72
West Lothian:
Tel: (050 682) 2330
Scenic upland course 3m N of Linlithgow off A706, 18 holes, 4600yds, par 63, SSS63

Riding
Edinburgh: Tower Farm Riding Stables, 85 Liberton Drive
Tel: 031-664 3375

General
Dunfermline:
Andrew Carnegie Birthplace: 19th-century cottage housing relics of the famous philanthropist
Open all year (ex Sun mornings)
Tel: (0383) 23638/ 24302
Dunfermline Abbey: Benedictine church located in Pittencrieff Park
Open all year
Edinburgh: Lauriston Castle: 16th-century mansion with fine antiques, NW of Edinburgh 1m E of Cramond
Open Apr–Oct daily (weekends only in winter)
Tel: 031-336 2060
Museum of Childhood: survey of children's life in the past
Open all year (ex Sun)
Linlithgow: Blackness Castle: 15th-century stronghold, formerly a prison
Open all year
Linlithgow Palace: fine ruins of 16th-century mansion with notable hall
Open all year
South Queensferry: William Sanderson & Son: whisky blending & bottling plant
Open all year (ex early Jul), tours by appointment only
Tel: 031-331 1500

Almondell and Calderwood Country Park
2m riverside/woodland trail. Start from south entrance, East Calder, 11m SW of Edinburgh off A71
Open all year

House of the Binns Woodland Walk
¾m through woods and farmland with fine views of River Forth. Start from track at junction of A904 and B9109, 7m W of South Queensferry
Open Easter–Sep daily 10–7 (ex Fri)

Water of Leith Walkway
7m trail following disused railway line along the Leith valley. Start beside the river at Balerno, 8m SW of Edinburgh off A70
Open all year

Torrance House Nature Trail

East Kilbride District Council,
Civic Centre, East Kilbride,
G74 1AB
Tel: East Kilbride (035 52) 28777

2 miles south of East Kilbride centre on the A726 to Strathaven

Map reference: NS655526

Approx 1-mile nature trail in wooded river valley in the grounds of 17th-century mansion

Facilities: Four illustrated brochures – one for each season; car park

Although East Kilbride is one of Scotland's newest towns, a satellite of Glasgow eight miles to the north west, its origins pre-date the Romans. Until the big expansion of 1947, it was a small village supported by a poor coal mining industry and successful shoe-making and muslin weaving trades with farmland devoted to dairy herds. The oldest building that survives is a crumbling, 16th-century building called Mains Castle; but two miles to the south, the grounds of Torrance House, built a century later, are very much alive.

As a very recent development, the local district council are turning two miles of the Rotten Calder (a tributary of the Calder) into a country park to be known as Calderglen. Threading through this heavily wooded valley is a three-quarters-of-a mile nature trail which follows the course of the river and returns on the opposite bank.

The dominant species of the wood is the beech, which opens its downy, pale leaves in spring and drops them, golden-brown in the autumn. Because the leaves do not rot easily, the ground is often several feet deep in a rustling carpet thick with triangular brown nuts. Dense foliage in high summer allows only a little sunlight through to dapple the forest floor, so few plants can grow. However, the leaves provide a sheltered habitat for colonies of insects, such as earthworms, beetles and snails, and the tiny creatures of the beechwood – woodmice, bank voles and even badgers.

Elsewhere, the smooth grey bark and jet black buds of ash appear. Unlike the beech, it opens its leaves late and sheds them early, so wild garlic, dog's mercury and wild arum get a chance to grow. The leaves decompose quickly and support a hoard of insects, but it is the bunches of yellow seeds, which look so much like old-fashioned keys, which keep small mammals and birds – particularly the bullfinch – alive throughout the winter. Moles abound in the woodland, attracted by the abundant insects.

On the river bank, the grass is a mass of yellow and pale orange wood avens, and the red-tinged leaves (and unpleasant smell) of herb Robert. Sticklebacks and minnows dart among the shallows. The underside of rocks are home to leeches, caddis flies and freshwater shrimps, and flying insects dance above the surface of the water.

The mixture of river and woodland attracts a cross-section of birds. The water-loving dipper walks upstream on the river bottom to find a meal of larvae and molluscs, while the long-beaked tree creeper spends its days winkling insects out of fissures in the bark of trees. Tits are common, somersaulting and defying gravity amongst mixed woodland – they, too, eat insects and nest wherever there is a natural hole in a tree. Their nests are skilfully composed of cobwebs and lichens and lined with feathers – building materials easily obtained along the trail. The damp, sheltered valley breeds several varieties of lichen and moss, and many of the trees are still green in winter. The colouring is that of polypody fern and not the tree's own leaves.

Like the trees and plants, the river changes with the seasons. In spring the level is high, swollen by melting ice and snow and each bend of the bank is alternately cut away or deposited with a mixture of sand and gravel. During a dry autumn, it is easy to study the confluence of the Rotten Burn and the Calder, as the tributary enters over a jumble of boulders and the remains of a bridge which was destroyed when the river was in flood. Winter arrives and the surface is plated with ice and once-dripping rocks hang with icicles. At this time of the year, the evergreens prevent the trail from looking too bare. The dark shiny leaves of rhododendron (probably cultivated initially

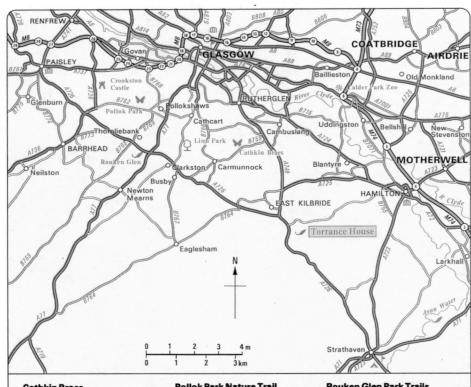

Cathkin Braes
½m upland trail. Start from Cathkin car park, 2m S of Rutherglen off B759
Open all year

Linn Park Nature Trail
3m woodland/riverside walk with varied flora. Start at Mansion House, 4m S of Glasgow off A727 (Clarkston Road) Open all year

Pollok Park Nature Trail
2m walk through copse with many flowering shrubs. Start at Pollok House, 5m SW of Glasgow off A736
Open all year

Rouken Glen Park Trails
Numerous walks through valley featuring lovely waterfall. Start from park entrance, ½m S of Thornliebank off B769
Open all year
Tel: 041-638 1077

but now wild and rampant), veined ivy and red-berried holly are reminders of Christmas decorations.

When snow covers the ground, animal tracks are more easily spotted and identified. Scotland is one of the last refuges of the red squirrel, but it will have hibernated at the first hint of cold weather, its cache of nuts safely stowed beneath an old tree trunk. Roe deer will make their delicate imprints on the forest floor, encouraged by the abundance of ferns and berries.

The end of the trail emerges in front of Torrance House. It was first owned by the Hamilton family and then by the Stuarts of Castlemilk and must have witnessed stormy clashes among the clans. Bonnie Prince Charlie is said to have spent the night there during his retreat from Derby in 1746.

East Kilbride boasts an impressive precinct, traffic-free with excellent shops and landscaped parks. Pride of all is an Olympic-sized swimming pool and leisure complex, incorporating Turkish baths and games facilities. The town also sports a windy parkland golf course but there is no shortage of good golfing opportunities anywhere in Scotland, especially around Glasgow.

Tributaries of the Clyde offer some scope for visiting anglers, although this great Scottish river is itself dogged by effluent, sewage and neglect in its lower reaches. The rivers Black Cart and Gryfe, which empty into the estuary near Renfrew, have trout (and the Gryfe, grayling, too). For seawater species, casting off the pier at Wemyss Bay hooks flat fish, cod and haddock.

The great explorer and missionary, David Livingstone, was born at Blantyre. His birthplace in Shuttle Row has been restored as a national museum and a memorial to his work in Africa. Another famous son of Scotland, Robert Burns, founded a literary and debating society at Tarbolton. The Bachelor's Club is commemorated each year on 25th January to which enthusiasts (men *and* women) are admitted. Burns would have approved, for the furnishings and décor inside the 17th-century thatched house are faithful reproductions.

At Uddington, Calderpark Zoo is a popular day out for both watching the animals and birds, walking round the reptile house and having a picnic on the grass. North of Glasgow is another area of country dedicated to walking, relaxing and enjoying the fresh air. Like Torrance House Nature Trail, it gives the impression of being in the heart of the Highlands, yet it is close to the centre of Glasgow.

Craigallian is covered by six miles of walks which thread across moor and grazing land and past the castles of Craigend and Mugdock. The mighty Mugdock reservoir ensures that Glasgow throats are never parched, and provides millions of gallons of water to the city.

Weaving kept the villagers of East Kilbride from poverty in the 18th century, and a typical weaver's cottage has been preserved as a museum at Kilbarchan. A 200-year-old loom is still operational, but in 1794, 383 looms would have clattered throughout the village producing lengths of cambric, lawns and tartans.

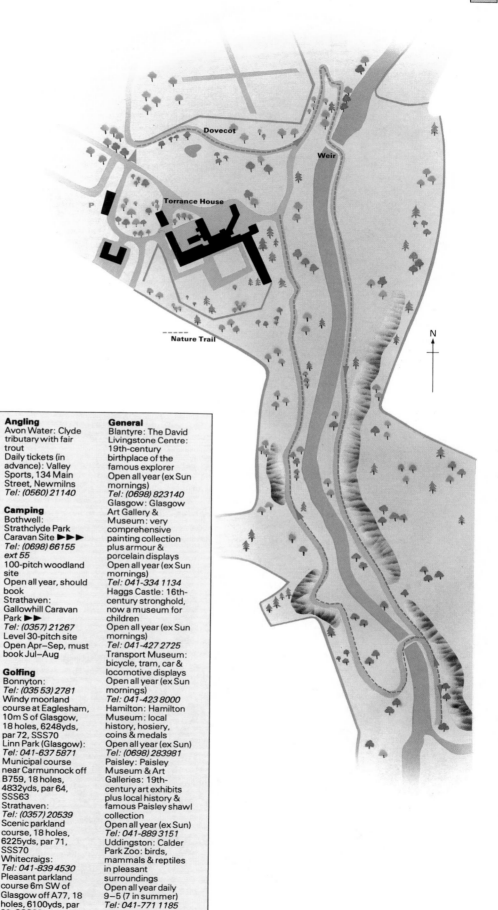

Angling
Avon Water: Clyde tributary with fair trout
Daily tickets (in advance): Valley Sports, 134 Main Street, Newmilns
Tel: (0560) 21140

Camping
Bothwell: Strathclyde Park Caravan Site ▶▶▶
Tel: (0698) 66155 ext 55
100-pitch woodland site
Open all year, should book
Strathaven: Gallowhill Caravan Park ▶▶
Tel: (0357) 21267
Level 30-pitch site
Open Apr–Sep, must book Jul–Aug

Golfing
Bonnyton:
Tel: (035 53) 2781
Windy moorland course at Eaglesham, 10m S of Glasgow, 18 holes, 6248yds, par 72, SSS70
Linn Park (Glasgow):
Tel: 041-637 5871
Municipal course near Carmunnock off B759, 18 holes, 4832yds, par 64, SSS63
Strathaven:
Tel: (0357) 20539
Scenic parkland course, 18 holes, 6225yds, par 71, SSS70
Whitecraigs:
Tel: 041-839 4530
Pleasant parkland course 6m SW of Glasgow off A77, 18 holes, 6100yds, par 69, SSS68

General
Blantyre: The David Livingstone Centre: 19th-century birthplace of the famous explorer
Open all year (ex Sun mornings)
Tel: (0698) 823140
Glasgow: Glasgow Art Gallery & Museum: very comprehensive painting collection plus armour & porcelain displays
Open all year (ex Sun mornings)
Tel: 041-334 1134
Haggs Castle: 16th-century stronghold, now a museum for children
Open all year (ex Sun mornings)
Tel: 041-427 2725
Transport Museum: bicycle, tram, car & locomotive displays
Open all year (ex Sun mornings)
Tel: 041-423 8000
Hamilton: Hamilton Museum: local history, hosiery, coins & medals
Open all year (ex Sun mornings)
Tel: (0698) 283981
Paisley: Paisley Museum & Art Galleries: 19th-century art exhibits plus local history & famous Paisley shawl collection
Open all year (ex Sun)
Tel: 041-889 3151
Uddingston: Calder Park Zoo: birds, mammals & reptiles in pleasant surroundings
Open all year daily 9–5 (7 in summer)
Tel: 041-771 1185

Island of Bute Natural History Trails

The Buteshire Natural History Society, The Museum, Stuart Street, Rothesay, Bute

> Bute is reached by regular vehicle ferry services Wemyss Bay – Rothesay and Colintraive – Rhubodach
>
> Map references:
>   Bull Loch Trail NS026744
>   South end of Bute Trail 5 NS106547
>
> Two of 7 trails around the island prepared by local natural historians: inland Bull Loch Trail—4-miles; coastal trail around south end of Bute (No. 5)—4 miles
>
> *Facilities:* Detailed trail booklets available from the Museum in Rothesay

Lying close to the fragmented coast of west Scotland, is the green and fertile Island of Bute. Smaller and softer-profiled than its rugged neighbour, Arran, Bute is covered by plantations and farmland, rich in natural history and archaeology and home of one of Scotland's foremost resorts, Rothesay.

Separating the island from the shore are the narrow Kyles of Bute, revered both for their beauty and excellence as sailing waters. So narrow are the Kyles (Gaelic for straits) between Colintraive and Rhubodach that at one time farmers forced their cattle to swim across

for St Blanes Fair on Bute. Today it is a five-minute crossing by car ferry, almost too quick to appreciate the stunning views. A longer crossing is from Wemyss Bay to Rothesay, or it is possible to board one of the cruise steamers that frequent the Clyde.

All roads on the island lead to Rothesay, and there are more in the dairy-farming south than in the north. Here walkers and naturalists can delight in exploring more vertical scenery on foot in the total peace of a countryside uncontaminated by exhaust fumes.

There are seven nature trails and descriptive booklets on each, produced by Buteshire Natural History Society, obtainable from the Bute Museum, Rothesay.

Where the ferry lands at Rhubodach and the A886 road from Rothesay terminates is where the Bull Loch Trail begins. It is about an hour's uphill climb to the loch itself, following bracken-massed sheep tracks, old paths or just a sense of direction. Walkers soon encounter Balnakailly burn, one of the many tiny waterways that rise in North Bute and flow out to the Kyles. At the mouth of this one are the rusting remains of the 'Snow-flight', a slate-carrying ship which collided with another boat in 1936. A few years later, during the Second World War a scheme was implemented which was to leave more chunks of iron littering the once-beautiful countryside.

To confuse the enemy, this part of western Scotland around the Clyde was festooned with lights so that in a black-out it would look like a built-up area. This northern half of Bute was banned to the public and used for commando training.

Years before, farmers worked the poor soil around Balnakailly and there are ruins of their houses. Cattle and sheep were fed on roots pounded into the hollow of a boulder with a

rock. One of these knocking stones lies among the grass at Balnakailly.

The surrounding woodlands are mainly lichen-covered oaks, witness to a damp atmosphere which encourages moss underfoot. It has proved to be a useful commodity. That pale moss, *Sphagnum*, was treated and used to pack wounds when cotton was scarce during the first war, and for years Bute's Girl Guides have gathered hair moss and sent it to a Poppy factory to back memorial wreaths of poppies.

Over the hillside, boots are scratched by three species of heather. *Erica tetralix* with its pale bells bunched at the top of the stem is the first to flower, followed by the larger bells of *Erica cinerea* (bell). In September, Bute like the rest of Scotland, is carpeted with the purple ling heather (*Calluna vulgaris*). Cotton grass loves boggy moorland (it, too, has been employed to stuff pillows and make candle wicks), as does the pale spotted orchid and the yellow-spiked bog asphodel.

At Bull Loch, the surface is curded with waterlilies and edged with reeds and sedges. Sightings of otter tracks have been reported on the steep muddy banks, but few walkers ever see this delightful animal. Overhead, birds of prey are common; the cream spotted underside of a kestrel catches the eye as it accelerates to catch a bird on the wing, and the slow-circular flight of a buzzard can quickly be converted into a downward plummet to devour a rabbit.

The loch can mark the end of the trail, but for a longer walk, the banks of a burn are followed through a boulder-strewn valley to the shore near the northern tip of the island.

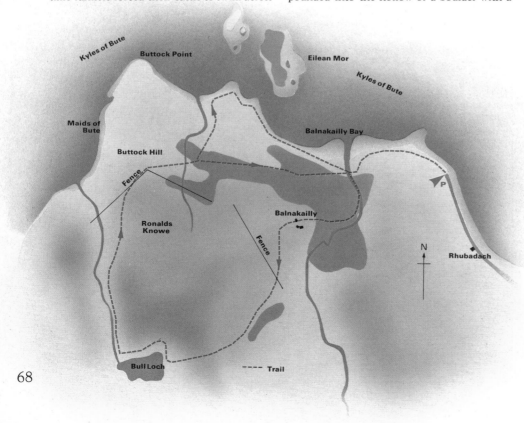

The path comes out near the Maids of Bute–two stones painted in red and white bands which look like sitting figures from the water. Oak trees grew along this shoreline and in the 19th century the bark was stripped off and used for tanning–a process long since superseded by modern chemicals.

Almost blocking the Kyles are a handful of small islets–the Burnt Islands which have been adopted by species of gulls. Herring, Common and the lesser Black-backed gulls nest untidily on the ground, with terns defending their brood aggressively a little later on. Sadly, these colonies are threatened by a contemptible but lucrative demand for sea birds' eggs. On the increase are eiderducks and swans nest here also. It is not uncommon to see the whiskery face of a seal pop out of the water somewhere around Burnt Islands.

Other islands in the Kyles have historic connections. To the north in Loch Ridden lies Eilean Dearg (One Tree Island) where the Campbells of Loch Awe built a castle and chapel in the 14th century. Three hundred years later, the 9th Duke of Argyll made Eilean Dearg his headquarters before the uprising of 1685. There is evidence that he did not do it alone, for recent excavations have unearthed Dutch muskets, flints and navigational dividers, suggesting the presence of William of Orange's men.

A fort on the Eilean Buidhe poses a mystery, for when it was excavated in 1936 the walls were found to be vitrified. It was as if exceptionally high temperatures had fused the stone together at some time in their history.

One clue may lie in the rock formations visible in the south of Bute. A nature trail which explores the coast and hills on a fist of land sticking out into the Firth of Clyde is geologically fascinating. Like the Loch Bull Trail, it begins where a road ends, at Kilchattan south of the B88.

Like the offshore island of Little Cumbrae, the south of Bute is made up of volcanic rock, columnar or jointed sandstone and basalt outcrops. The shore is remarkable for another phenomenon, a good example of a raised beach, some twenty-five feet higher than the present level. This makes a natural highway for walkers who can discover the caves which pockmark the old red sandstone cliffs. A cave on Creag a Mhara headland was excavated, but only shells and animal bones were found and no human artefacts.

From the unattended lighthouse at Rhun an Ean (the point of the birds), there are breathtaking views of Great and Little Cumbrae and glimpses of the Ayrshire coast beyond. The sea teems with fish, so heron are regular anglers, and basking sharks, seals and porpoises are not uncommon.

After passing a Bronze Age cairn and the ruins of an inn which accommodated sailors awaiting fair winds to Ireland or America, the trail turns away from the sea and climbs upward. Loch na Leigh (the physician's loch or pool of healing) is a sanctuary for nesting seabirds, tufted ducks and teals. The waters are edged with the velvet batons of bulrush and colourful bog plants and the air is full of a variety of bird song.

Equally idyllic is the 17th-century chapel of St Blane, built among cliffs and trees overlooking the sea on the site of a tiny church founded in the 6th century. The trail booklet devotes several pages to this, the highspot of the walk and to the fascinating relics which mark centuries of use by a religious community. The walk back to Kilchattan follows the old track made by villagers coming over Suidhe Hill to worship at St Blanes. It is rarely dry underfoot, with grass and gorse bushes cropped by sheep and swaths of bracken, but the view from the hill, 'the seat of the King', 516ft above the sea, is one of the best on the island.

Another trail leading to St Blanes begins at Kingarth cemetery and passes through farmland, plantations and the vitrified fort of Dunagoil. Of historical interest are groups of Bronze Age standing stones, foundations of two Norse long-houses and the earliest type of Neolithic burial chamber.

There are more of these chambers on a trail which sets off from the sandy bay at Ettrick and leads north for about three hours to Kilmichael chapel. More evidence of Bute's volcanic and glacial history can be seen, but more impressive are the traces left by early man–the oldest, at around 3000 BC, is at Glecknabae Cairn.

Even Bute's capital and popular resort, Rothesay, has its own walkabouts. One goes round the bay, the hub of the town which at one time was busy with trading ships. Today the harbour is packed with the tall sails of private yachts and it has become a major sailing centre in addition to being a popular stopping-off point for the frequent Clyde steamer tours.

Another route leads up the High Street and to the ruins of the round castle. Begun in the early 13th century, it was stormed by the Vikings, took a punishing in the Civil War and was burned by the Duke of Argyll in 1685. However, much of it remains, thanks to renovations carried out by the second and third marquesses of Bute, and both the castle and Rothesay's fortunes are traced and catalogued in the museum nearby. Apart from tourism, Rothesay has thriving cheese-making and woven cloth industries. Bute Creamery is built over a stone-age village and Bute Looms is housed in a former convent and cotton mill.

Another way of exploring the island is by car, and this is possible by following a five-point route which takes about two hours. This way, an overall impression is gained, banks of wild flowers become a coloured haze and individual fields melt into a tapestry of rolling farmland. From Rothesay, the motorist visits Craigmore, Kerrycroy, Kingarth, Scalpsie Bay, Ettrick Bay and Port-Bannatyne.

Across the Kyles to the north of Bute, the rugged terrain is covered with mixed wood plantations, many of them planted by the Forestry Commission quite recently. The older trees surround what used to be the laird's house in the former Caladh estate. The trail has some steep, slippery sections in countryside inhabited by wild cats, badgers and foxes, although a roebuck is more often glimpsed through the trees on a summer day. The castle itself was demolished unceremoniously when it was found to have terminal dry rot, and only the landscaped gardens remain. They contain flowering shrubs and specimen trees planted by the various owners of the house, which included George Stephenson, nephew of the railway pioneer. A waterlily-covered pond is the quiet water hole for a number of wild fowl and creatures from the forest, and a natural harbour behind the tiny island Eilean Dubh, has long been a refuge for yachtsmen.

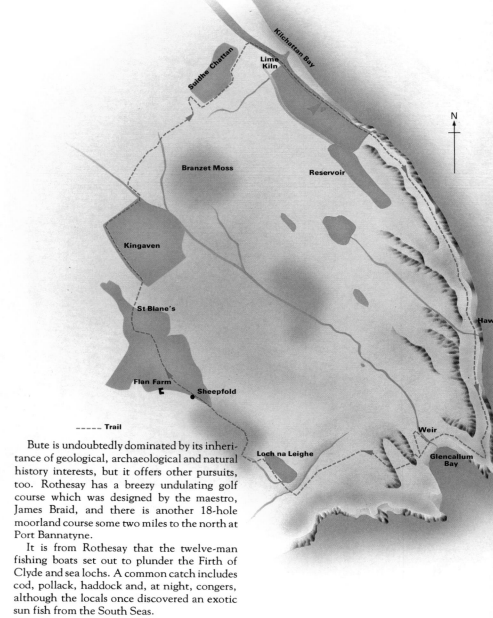

----- Trail

Bute is undoubtedly dominated by its inheritance of geological, archaeological and natural history interests, but it offers other pursuits, too. Rothesay has a breezy undulating golf course which was designed by the maestro, James Braid, and there is another 18-hole moorland course some two miles to the north at Port Bannatyne.

It is from Rothesay that the twelve-man fishing boats set out to plunder the Firth of Clyde and sea lochs. A common catch includes cod, pollack, haddock and, at night, congers, although the locals once discovered an exotic sun fish from the South Seas.

Angling
Rothesay: excellent shore fishing for cod, mackerel & pollock. Plus coalfish, whiting & wrasse by boat

Camping
Sandbank: Cot House Garage ▶
Tel: (036 984) 351
Coastal 15-pitch site 4m N of Dunoon
Open Apr–Oct, no bookings

Golfing
Kyles of Bute: exposed moorland course 1m S of Tighnabruaich off B8000, 9 holes, 2379yds, par 32
Port Bannatyne: hilly seaside course 2m NW of Rothesay off A844, 18 holes, 5500yds, par 67, SSS63

General
Kilchattan: St Blane's Chapel: well-
preserved Celtic site, 2m S of Kilchattan
Accessible all year
Millport: Museum of the Cumbraes: photographs & relics depicting local life, on Gt Cumbrae Island east of Bute
Open 10–4.30 during summer (ex Sun & Mon), plus other times by appointment
Tel: (047 553) 741
Rothesay: Bute Museum: natural history, bygones & archaeology
Open all year (Mon–Sat afternoons only in winter)
Rothesay Castle: 13th-century fortress with circular courtyard
Open all year
Rothesay Tourist organisation: further details of things to do on Bute, at The Pier, Rothesay
Tel: (0700) 2151

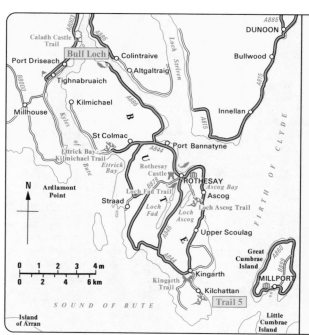

Caladh Castle Trail
1½m forest walk with fine views of the Kyles of Bute. Start at Caladh, 3m NE of Tighnabruaich off A8003
Open all year

Ettrick Bay-Kilmichael Trail
6m coastal walk of archaeological interest. Start at bus stop, Ettrick Bay
Open all year

Kingarth Trail
5m trail rich in flora. Start from Kingarth churchyard, 7m S of Rothesay off A844
Open all year

Loch Ascog Trail
3m walk from Ascog Bay to Rothesay via loch. Start at Ascog Bay off A844
Open all year

Loch Fad Trail
4½m lochside trail. Start from Bute Museum, Rothesay
Open all year

Arbroath Cliffs Nature Trail

The Scottish Wildlife Trust,
Dundee and Angus Branch,
The Secretary, 2 Castle Street,
Forfar

The De'il's Heid

Trail starts at St Ninian's Well at the east end of Arbroath sea front promenade

Map reference: NO659412

3-mile clifftop footpath walk with one avoidable steep section exploring cliff and rock flora and sea birds

Facilities: Illustrated trail brochure from Trust or local tourist office; car park on sea front

World-famous for its smokies, the Royal Burgh of Arbroath is a popular seaside resort and a busy fishing port with a higher summer sunshine record than the coastal towns on the west coast of Scotland.

Built among ruddy-red cliffs of sandstone, the town has a long and rich history. It was an early Pictish settlement, and in 1178 King William the Lion founded the abbey which was later dedicated to St Thomas à Becket. The year 1320 saw Robert Bruce signing Scotland's Declaration of Independence here, and over six hundred years later the Stone of Scone was discovered in the ruins of the abbey, after it

had been removed from beneath the Coronation Chair in Westminster Abbey. The town's former, unabbreviated name, Aberbrothock (so-called because of its position at the mouth of Brothock Water), is immortalised in Southey's poem *The Inchcape Rock* and, disguised as *Fairport*, it features largely in Sir Walter Scott's *The Antiquary*.

For the golfing enthusiast, there is the challenge of the Championship Course (and an easier one) at Carnoustie, while the walker and explorer can plunder the treasures of an enchanting three-mile nature trail and the magnetism of caves along the coast.

The trail begins at the north end of the promenade, where there is ample space for parking the car. As this is a clifftop walk, any detour from the footpath could be dangerous; at places the sea pounds far inland into underground caves and crevices, and the turf underfoot can be slippery.

For miles along this Angus coast, the rocks form a mighty red cliff which can be seen from a boat several miles out to sea on a clear day. This sandstone is pock-marked with round pebbles in patches and cracked or faulted in others, so there is a fascinating variety of formations and flora to please the geologist and the botanist. Where the clifftop is speckled with stones, lime-loving clustered bell-flower and Carline thistle grow and the beach beneath is pebbly. Where the faults and weakness occur, the sea has taken advantage, and whipped the rock into pinnacles, arches and coves.

In the salty air it is not only the maritime plants that flourish. Sea plantain, sea campion and scurvy grass are there by rights, but it is surprising to see the delicate primrose, violet

and early purple orchis, which normally confine themselves to woodlands. Like the green-veined white, common blue and small heath butterflies that are a common sight, these non-maritime plants are happy in an environment where they are not crushed by human traffic, sprayed with weedkiller or munched by grazing cattle.

Springs of fresh water, like those at the beginning of the trail and at St Ninian's Well, are flanked by marshy ground in which the vibrant purple marsh orchis, meadow-sweet and meadow cranes-bill appear. High on the clifftop, the ground is a profusion of powder-blue harebells, purple milk-vetch and sea-pinks in summer. Different species of snail can also be spotted: from the brown-banded pale pink or yellow shells of *Cepaea hortensis*, which is found well-camouflaged among fallen leaves among the rocks, to the brown or yellow mottled *Arianta arbustorum*, which likes nettles. Less common are the tiny *Helicella virgata*, which resemble pearl shirt buttons, found among the moss and short grass.

Common to the entire coastline of Scotland, and visible at several points along Arbroath's Cliff trail, are raised beaches. Formed many thousands of years ago around the end of the last Ice Age, these platforms of springy turf were once lapped by the sea until the land was

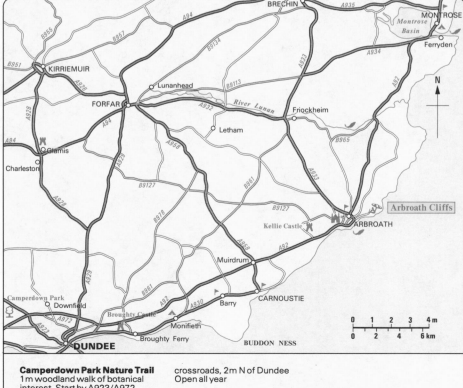

Camperdown Park Nature Trail
1m woodland walk of botanical interest. Start by A923/A972

crossroads, 2m N of Dundee
Open all year

72

their constant and desperate search for food.

The trail takes about two hours to complete, but longer if specimens are collected. Rock-pools give hours of diversion. Small black crabs skulk under squeaky tresses of bladderwrack, while barnacles and limpets stick fast to the rocks. The fresh green fans of sea lettuce grow profusely in summer, sometimes obscuring the red wine-gum-like beadlet sea anemone. The pebbles on the beach are derived from various types of rock from the Highland region and are older than the surrounding sandstone. Mottled pink or grey stones are granite and translucent fawn or grey pebbles are likely to be quartzite. Self-coloured or veined varieties of red, green and lavender can also be found.

A collection of larger stones, sculptured by generations of craftsmen from early Christian and mediaeval periods is on show at St Vigeans museum, and includes the Drosten Stone.

Only the south transept gable and the west front remain of the once-magnificent Tironensian Abbey at Arbroath, but the abbot's house, intact with a 12th-century kitchen, is well-preserved and open as a museum. The town's Signal Tower museum covers a wider history of local natural history and there is also an art gallery with a fine gallery of pastels and watercolours by J W Herald.

Also in ruins is Red Castle, an austere 15th-century edifice of red sandstone which probably replaced a defence stronghold of an earlier period against raids by Danish pirates. Kelly Castle, south of Arbroath, is genuinely ancient, with parts dating back to 1170. It has been imaginatively and skilfully converted into a modern home, and some of the rooms house a gallery of Scottish arts. Here artists and craftsmen from anywhere in Scotland can exhibit and sell their work.

Miles of sand, safe-bathing beaches and indoor and outdoor swimming pools make Arbroath a popular seaside resort. It is a favourite spot with anglers, too. Codling, plaice and flounder are common catches from the shore, and from a boat there is a good chance of cod, mackerel, pollack and, naturally, haddock. As smoking is still a cottage industry, it is possible to get a private catch cooked this way.

With such a sea harvest, it is small wonder that the cliffs of Arbroath are haunted with the plaintive cry of seagulls.

elevated. Rising up behind these one-time beaches are the old sea cliffs, now covered with bracken, briar and blackthorn with patches of cow parsley, red campion and the ubiquitous nettle. The most outstanding geological phenomenon of this stretch of coast is the number of sea-sculpted formations. Needle E'e is a fine example of a natural arch, running parallel, not as is usual, at right angles, to the shoreline. One day the sea will probably erode away the arch itself, in the same way as it has reduced a cave system at Seaman's Grave to an untidy tip of boulders and rubble. Mason's cave is one of the largest caverns, and undoubtedly used for smuggling – it is near an ancient earthwork called Maiden Castle.

Here and there an outcrop of sandstone has been left stranded several feet from the shore, as at De'il's Heid (also called Pint Stoup or The Poll). Obviously composed of a much harder sandstone than the surrounding cliffs, in common with an isolated stack at the entrance to Dickmont's Den, it is the perfect sanctuary for colonies of sea birds.

Herring gulls, fulmars and terns wheel and cry over the cliffs and build their ragged nests wherever there is a ledge. Tiny crevices and dark caves appeal to house martins and rock doves, while out at sea, stripey-beaked puffins, guillemots and cormorants skim the water in

To Arbroath-Auchmithie Road

To Auchmithie

Dark Cave

Carlinghuegh Bay

The Three Sisters

Cove Haven

Maiden Castle

N

The De'il's Heid

Dickmont's Den

The Blow-hole

The Crusie

Seaman's Grave

The Mermaid's Kirk

The Needle E'e

Nature Trail

Other Paths

To Arbroath Town Centre

Promenade

St Ninian's Well

Whiting Ness

Glamis Castle Nature Trail

Strathmore Estates Ltd, Estates Office, Glamis, Angus, DD8 1RQ
Tel: Glamis (030 784) 242

Off A928 4 miles south of Kirriemuir close to junction with A94 at village of Glamis

Map reference: N0387480

½-mile trail viewing superb mature trees and parkland wildlife in grounds of historic castle—good access for disabled visitors

Facilities: Illustrated trail guide; car park; tours of castle

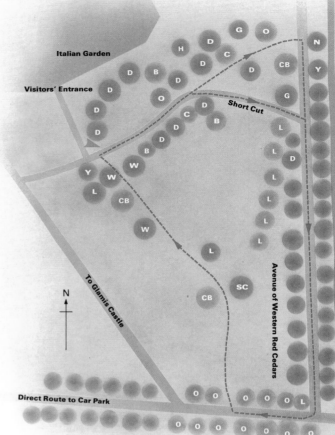

Broadleaf Trees

- **B** Beech
- **L** Lime
- **CB** Copper Beech
- **S** Sycamore
- **O** Oak
- **C** Sweet Chestnut

Conifers

- **D** Douglas Fir
- **G** Giant Fir
- **N** Noble Fir
- **W** Western Hemlock
- **L** Larch
- **SC** Sawara Cypress
- **W** Western Red Cedar
- **Y** Yew

Probably the most famous village in Angus is Glamis, dominated by an imposing castle, the home of the Earls of Strathmore and Kinghorne. It is believed that a fortification of some kind has stood on this site since time immemorial, at least since 1034 when Malcolm II died here. Today's structure is 14th century, with late 17th century additions and embellishments to resemble a French château.

The building stone used was locally-quarried pink sandstone. Only Duncan's Hall, said to be the setting for Shakespeare's Macbeth, Thane of Glamis, and the fifteen-foot-thick walls of the square tower are original.

From the windows of the upper floor and the battlements is a beautiful view of the fertile Vale of Strathmore and elaborate gardens below, which contain an enormous sundial.

Glamis was the childhood home of Queen Elizabeth, the Queen Mother, and the birthplace of Princess Margaret in 1930. The castle's Royal connections had a more turbulent history in 1537 when Janet, Lady of Glamis was burnt at the stake for witchcraft and for conspiring to murder James V. The castle was forfeited to the crown, which is why the Royal coat of arms surmounts the entrance door beside those of the Lyon's.

Inside, fine panelled walls are graced by tapestries, antique furniture and paintings and collections of china and armour. In the

grounds is something very new—the castle's first nature trail.

In common with other landowners, Strathmore Estate fells trees once they have reached the right specifications for sale. Gone is the demand for the giant, straight trunks of the Douglas fir to make masts for sailing ships. Modern plantations are of quick-growing conifers for paper and larch for fencing panels. Along this half-mile trail, at least, the glorious, if uneconomic, specimen trees remain to delight the walker.

Following well-defined paths, it is impossible not to recognise the massive dark bulk of Douglas firs, some of them over a hundred years old. The ground underfoot is littered by their long, bracted cones. Although the larch also has cones, it is one of the few deciduous conifers. For although its tiny needles break fresh green each spring, they turn yellow and fall to the ground in late autumn. Most woodlands of any great age contain a yew tree or two. The hard, yet malleable wood has always been prized, especially for making long bows and furniture. Here at Glamis there are both male trees, covered in cream pollen cones during the winter, and female trees, identifiable in autumn by their succulent-looking red berries. Picking them is a temptation to be avoided, for all the tree is poisonous.

There are broadleaves too, such as the vibrant beech which turns into many shades of gold in October, or its elegant cousin, the copper beech, resplendent in a cloak of burnished bronze. *Quercus robur* makes a better specimen oak than *Quercus petraea*, for the leaves have short stalks, yet the acorns stick out on long twigs. Like the sycamore, oaks spread their seedlings wide, and the forest floor erupts with tiny bonsai-like trees each summer.

Fighting for space and daylight are ground cover plants such as rhododendrons, which break into a mass of scented colour each June. Along the trail are banks of dog's mercury and forget-me-not and another plant not so easily recognised. Tuberous comfrey, with its bristly-veined leaves and drooping clusters of pale flowers, is seldom found outside Angus, although here it is a common woodland dweller.

Only the fortunate few spot the ruddy-red coat of a roe deer as it skips through the forest. Far more common, although not to those south of the border, is the glimpse of a red squirrel as it jumps between the trees like a trapeze artist. Parts of Scotland are still without the larger, more aggressive grey squirrel which was introduced from North America at the expense of our native variety and our woodlands.

Even without seeing the source, the noises of the wood can be recognised. The gentle coo-ing of the woodpigeon is rudely interrupted by the staccato drilling of a greater-spotted woodpecker, or the mocking laugh of another member of the family, the green woodpecker. A rustle in the undergrowth or a narrow track among the grass is a give-away that a rabbit's burrow is near. With the large families that Glamis' woods support and an energetic mole population, walking amongst the woodlands off the beaten track without due care could result in a sprained ankle.

Glamis Castle

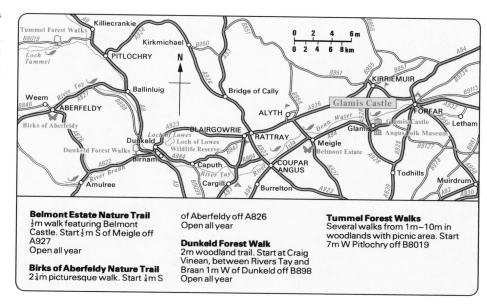

Belmont Estate Nature Trail
½m walk featuring Belmont Castle. Start ½m S of Meigle off A927
Open all year

Birks of Aberfeldy Nature Trail
2¼m picturesque walk. Start ¼m S

of Aberfeldy off A826
Open all year

Dunkeld Forest Walk
2m woodland trail. Start at Craig Vinean, between Rivers Tay and Braan 1m W of Dunkeld off B898
Open all year

Tummel Forest Walks
Several walks from 1m–10m in woodlands with picnic area. Start 7m W Pitlochry off B8019

The trail skirts Glamis burn, which is stocked with brown and rainbow trout and inhabited by pairs of mallards, coots and water-hens. Occasionally a long-legged heron will visit the burn to fish, and there is always a chance of seeing the brilliant electric-blue flash of a darting kingfisher.

The region around Glamis, north of Dundee is a rich, fertile belt of land where miles are sown to arable crops and cereals. It is famous for seed potatoes and the soft fruits which ripen in a trough of sheltered countryside are sent to the restaurants of Edinburgh and further south.

One side of the Glamis estate is bordered by the Water of Dean, a tributary of the Isla which links this river with Glamis. The rewards of fishing it are similar to those of nearby Kerbet Water, trout and grayling.

In the village of Glamis, a low-slung terrace of 17th-century stone cottages have been converted into a museum of local domestic and agricultural life up to the 19th century. Near Kirkwynd Cottages in the manse garden is the Malcolm Stone, said to be the gravestone of King Malcolm II. Experts set the date much earlier, at around 9th–10th century.

One of Scotland's best-loved story-tellers, author of *Peter Pan*, J M Barrie was born in a small house at Kerriemuir. Today Number 9, Brechin Road is a museum full of his personal mementoes and early jottings.

Like Glamis Castle, Forfar, the county town of Angus, has a violent history. The town hall has preserved the Forfar bridle, an iron collar with a prong which was used to silence witches during torture and persecution. The shores of the Forfar Loch were the battlefields of Picts and Scots for the last time before the kingdoms were at last united.

Less bloodthirsty, the son of the king who died at the site of Glamis Castle, Malcolm II, obviously had a penchant for fish, for a track known as King's Codger's Road once ran from Forfar east to the sea at Usan. By foot or pony, this ensured the king of a ready supply of fresh fish. His castle (and his kitchens) were destroyed by Robert the Bruce, who in turn buried his son at Restenneth Priory. Today

only ruins remain of a once-substantial retreat built by Augustinian canons, although the lofty square tower could have been standing since the 11th century.

Scotland's high reputation for golf courses is upheld by lovely views and mixed parkland and heathland underfoot at Kirriemuir, a windy day's sport at Alyth or a choice of three sites at Blairgowrie, further away. Less purposeful, but still rewarding, with fine views, is a walk over the Hill of Finavon, north east of Forfar.

Angling
River Isla: good trout & grayling
Free fishing beyond Airlie Castle
Further information: Tay Salmon Fisheries Board (Water Bailiff), Alyth
Tel: (082 83) 3239
Kerbet Water, small game fishing stream off Water of Dean (see below)
Daily tickets (in advance): C Kerr, 1 West High Street, Forfar
Tel: (0307) 73347
Water of Dean: good trout stream linking with the River Isla at Glamis Castle
Daily tickets: as Kerbet Water

Camping
Cargill: Beech Hedge Restaurant & Caravan Park ►►
Tel: (025 083) 249
Partly sloping 8-pitch site 6m S of Blairgowrie off A93
Open all year, must book Jul–Aug
Forfar: Lochside Caravan Park ►►
Tel: (0307) 2528
Mainly level 48-pitch site (no tents)
Open Apr–Oct, must book Jul–Aug

Golfing
Alyth:
Tel: (082 83) 268
Breezy moorland

course, 18 holes, 6203yds, par 70, SSS70
Blairgowrie:
Tel: (0250) 2622
Two heathland courses, 18 holes, 6592yds (6621), par 72 (71), SSS72 (72)
Forfar:
Tel: (0307) 2120
Picturesque moorland course, 18 holes, 6218yds, par 69, SSS69
Kirriemuir:
Tel: (057 52) 2144
Parkland/heathland course, 18 holes, 5470yds, par 68, SSS67

General
Dunkeld: Loch of Lowes Wildlife Reserve: variety of wildfowl plus displays, 2m NE of Dunkeld
Open Apr–Sep
Tel: (035 02) 337
Glamis: Angus Folk Museum: row of cottages housing agricultural & domestic exhibits
Open May–Sep daily 1–6
Kirriemuir: Barrie's Birthplace: small house containing relics & mementoes of the writer Sir James Barrie
Open May–Sep (ex Sun mornings), or by appointment
Tel: (057 52) 2646

Glencoe Forest Trails

Forestry Commission, Forest Office, Glenachulish, Argyll
Tel: Ballachulish (085 52) 268

Trails centred on Glencoe village on A82 Tyndrum–Kinlochleven road

Map references:
   Signal Rock Trail NN129565
   Lochan Forest Trail NN099588

Two trails in small woodlands at mouth of historic Glencoe:
Signal Rock Trail—about 1¼ miles;
Lochan Trail—about 2 miles

Facilities: Illustrated trail booklet; car parks; visitor centres; cafés in village

Nestled in the wildly beautiful region of the old Argyll border with Inverness, is the village of Glencoe, just inland from the lovely Loch Leven. This very old crofting community lies on the main road through the glen and is hemmed in on three sides by mountains. The 2430ft Pap of Glencoe, to the east, is the most imposing mountain in the area with its strange conical peak.

In most people's minds this area is associated with just one thing—the Glencoe Massacre, a macabre event in Scottish history. It was along this craggy valley on a fateful February day in 1692 that some forty members of the Macdonald clan, having offered Robert Campbell and his troops twelve days' hospitality, were mercilessly slaughtered in their own homes. The clan's lateness in swearing allegiance to the new king, William III, was used as a pretext for the atrocity. A monument, erected in 1883, stands at the end of the main street near the ruins of the very cottages in which the gory deed took place so long ago.

At the western end of the village is the only car park. From here it is a walk of just under half a mile to the Lochan Forest Trail. Turn left over the River Coe, pass on through the grounds of Glencoe Hospital, where an eventual sharp right leads into Glencoe Forest via an ingenious deer-proof gate. Despite this barrier there are, in fact, some twenty resident roe deer. The blunted tips of the saplings are evidence of the environmental damage that these lovely, but troublesome creatures cause.

The Forestry Commission has been very active within this trail since their first plantings of 1922. Spruce, pine and larch are now the principal species, interspersed by naturally regenerative ash, plus the older hazel and sycamore surviving on the hillside.

Where the path approaches Loch Leven, you can look down on Eilean Munde (the Burial Islands), on which all local Camerons and Macdonalds were at one time interred. On the mainland to the left is the abandoned site of a once-thriving slate quarry. Just beyond is

Glencoe

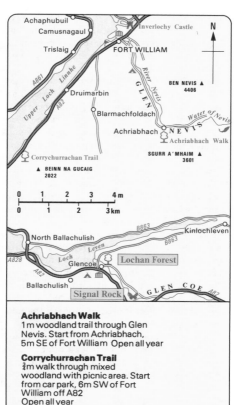

Ballachulish, a small town formerly dependent on the slate industry, but recently emerging as a tourist spot. If you strain your eyes to still further west, you should be able to follow the course of the mist-enshrouded Loch Linnhe.

Badgers abound along this coastal stretch of the walk, but are only to be espied at dawn and twilight. Their tracks, however, can be traced where they have disturbed the soil during one of their foraging sorties.

Where the path runs adjacent to the A82, further deer vandalism is apparent on studying the western red cedar. Many birds nest in these tall trees, including rooks, thrushes, crows and the occasional buzzards. Any hole you spot in an alder tree here may turn out to be a wren community's roost, as these tiny birds tend to huddle together on cold nights.

Towards the end of this circular walk, with the eastern landscape now totally dominated by the Pap of Glencoe, there is an artificial lake, 'the Lochan', which gives the trail its name. The water was formed by damming and flooding an old peat bog. An offshoot of the main trail circumvents the loch, and the June-flowering rhododendrons plus the chance of an otter sighting should be sufficient incentive to go the long way. At the point where this path rejoins the trail proper, an old boathouse serves as a resting place for those with weary limbs. As an ending to the two-mile trail, there are dozens of plants set in a natural garden surrounding a lily pond.

Once back at Glencoe village, Signal Rock trail is only two miles away to the south east. off the A82, midway between the two trails, is the wood-encircled Glencoe Campsite. Across the nearby River Coe is a youth hostel. The small beach between these two stop-overs makes this area very popular.

There are several means of access to this second forest trail, but the Glencoe Visitor Centre on the A82 roadside, with its information bureau and parking facilities, is obviously a preferable starting point.

Two lofty mounds rising from the glen are the walk's main features. Tom a' Ghrianain (Signal Rock) was once believed to have religious connections, but nowadays is regarded as the spot where the Glencoe Massacre signal was given, hence the name. The other knoll is called An Torr and, like its neighbour, affords marvellous glenland views.

Signal Rock can only be approached via private property and consequently all walkers are requested to keep strictly to the path. There are remains of an early house here, which dates back to before the Massacre.

Much of this trail is set in woodland and is also protected by a deer fence. The region provides shelter for many animals including fox, rabbit and wild mink. Birdlife, too, is abundant. Specialised Forestry Commission leaflets, available from the Visitor Centre, will help you to study the trail's flora and fauna in more depth—especially the many species of trees, some of which are individually numbered for quick reference.

Back at the roadside is a huge heather-bound boulder, reputed to be R L Stevenson's inspiration for a hiding place needed by the characters

in *Kidnapped*, his classic adventure novel. At a leisurely stroll, allow forty-five minutes for this one-and-a-half-mile trail.

In Glencoe itself, housed in two thatched cottages along the one main throughfare, is an interesting folk museum. As well as many relics of the Jacobites and the Macdonalds, you can browse through local domestic and farming exhibits. To the north at Fort William, the West Highland Museum has displays on a similar theme. Fortress buffs should be impressed by Inverlochy Castle, whilst golfers will find

the town's scenic moorland course at Torlundy the only oasis in an otherwise rather barren golfing area.

Running south east from Fort William, the crystal-clear Water of Nevis provides anglers with fine salmon and sea trout sport during the summer months. The river springs, as its name implies, from the slopes of Ben Nevis. Numerous walkways are etched across the foothills of Scotland's highest mountain, but further in-roads on this peak should only be undertaken by experienced walkers and climbers.

Angling
Water of Nevis: mountain stream offering good salmon & sea trout
Daily tickets (in advance): Tackle Shop, Fort William
Tel: (0397) 2656

Camping
Fort William: Glen Nevis Caravan & Camping Park ►►►
Tel: (0397) 2191
Scenic 350-pitch site (120 caravans)
Open Mar–Sep, no bookings
Glencoe: Glencoe Campsite ►►►
Tel: (085 52) 397
Partly sloping 218-pitch site (108 tents)
Open mid-Dec–Sep, no bookings
Invercoe Caravan Site ►►
Tel: (085 52) 210
Partly sloping 280-pitch site (108 tents)
Open Easter–Oct, no

bookings

Golfing
Fort William:
Tel: (0397) 4464
Moorland course with good views, 18 holes, 5566yds, par 69, SSS68

General
Fort William: Inverlochy Castle: well-preserved 13th-century fortress Viewable at all times
West Highland Museum: wildlife, geology & archaeology plus Jacobite exhibits
Open mid-Jun–mid-Sep (ex Sun) 9.30–9, until 5 in winter
Glencoe: Glencoe & North Lorn Folk Museum: domestic & agricultural exhibits plus Macdonald & Jacobite items
Open mid-May–Sep 10–5.30 (ex Sun)

Achriabhach Walk
1m woodland trail through Glen Nevis. Start from Achriabhach, 5m SE of Fort William Open all year

Corrychurrachan Trail
¾m walk through mixed woodland with picnic area. Start from car park, 6m SW of Fort William off A82
Open all year

----- Lochan Trail
——— Forestry Commission

Signal Rock Trail -----
Forestry Commission ———

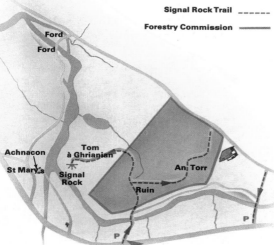

Glen More and Loch an Eilein Nature Trails

Glen More Forest Trails, Forestry Commission, Glen More Information Centre, Aviemore, Highland
Tel: Cairngorm (047 986) 271

Glen More Trail
On ski road off B970 (at Coylumbridge) 6 miles east of Aviemore

Map reference: NH974095

Three trails displaying both modern forestry techniques and natural Cairngorm flora and fauna: Shore Trail – 1¼ miles; River trail – 3 miles; Pinewood Trail – 1¼ miles

Facilities: Illustrated trail brochure covering all three trails; Visitor Centre; picnic areas; car parks; campsite

Loch an Eilein Trail
Nature Conservancy Council Visitor Centre, Kinakyle, Aviemore, Highland
Tel: Aviemore (0479) 810250

3 miles south of Aviemore off B970

Map reference: NH898084

3-mile trail around typical small Scottish loch once used as a timber-gathering pool – nearby are possible Iron Age settlements

Facilities: Illustrated trail brochure; car park; Visitor Centre

---

Between Aviemore and Braemar rises the largest tract of mountainous land of over 3000-feet in Britain – the Cairngorms. The high, Cairngorm plateau forms a broad, undulating range broken by four of the five highest peaks in the country and bordered by vertical cliff faces and cauldron-like corries. Steep-sided glens, deepened by glacial action, are entrenched into the plateau, fast-flowing mountain streams and waterfalls tumble over the the rockface and deep, well-hidden lochs and corrie lakes glisten in the sunlight. The dramatic outline of the mountains in contrast with the steep valleys gives the landscape its unique and splendid character.

The Cairngorm mountains stand prominently beside the neighbouring hills, for their granite construction has proved the more resilient to the ravages of time and weather. It was the pink felspars found within the granite that first gave rise to the old name for the Cairngorms, the Monadh Ruadh or Red Mountains.

Natural pine forest originally extended along the length of the entire Spey Valley and crept slowly into the tributaries and across the mountain slopes creating an impenetrable blanket of Caledonian pines. During the intervening centuries, the need for timber depleted the forest and little now remains. However, concealed within the stronghold of one such valley lies the Glen More Forest Park – 4000 acres of thick woodland, forest and heath surrounding the sandy shores of Loch Morlich.

Lacing through the south part of the woods, the Queen's Forest, the Forestry Commission has established three trails. The first takes in much of the shore of Loch Morlich and is linked to the second, the Pinewood Trail, by a bridge over the Allt Mhor river (Great River) feeding the lake. The River Trail takes a tour around the woods of the Allt Mhor and Allt na Ciste valleys. All the walks are graded as easy – the Shore and Pinewood Trails are each only one-and-a-quarter miles long, while the Riverside Trail is three miles long. The trails are loops starting close to the Glen More Forest Park information centre and campsite.

Early records show that Glen More was once used as a hunting forest, first for the Stewarts of Kincardine, then for the Kings of Scotland and later for the Dukes of Gordon. In addition, the tenants of the Gordon estates were granted the privilege of collecting 'torch wood' and were allowed limited pasturage. Although at

Loch Morlich, Glen More

the time it was a punishable offence, there is little doubt that the tenants stripped the bark to provide dyes for tanning and for roof cover.

The Spey Valley was immensely rich in timber resources and despite the difficult transport problems involved, was readily exploited for its riches.

In the 17th century, a tenant could harvest timber – provided he used only a saw and an axe – for an annual rent of 25p and a pound of tobacco. By 1766 the price for a butt had risen to 16p and felling reached an astounding level. Records for a Cairngorm estate of that period show the timber contract amounted to the staggering sum of £7000. The logs were drawn by horses to the banks of the forest streams, peeled and allowed to dry naturally and, when conditions were favourable, floated down the Druie and Sluggan to join the Spey. Here, a mass of logs were joined together with horsehair ropes and the resultant raft guided down to the sawmills by a system of ropes and by one man travelling alongside in a small coracle. The timber was utilised by local boatyards or alternatively the trunks were bored out and shipped to London for use as pipes in the new water-supply systems.

Glen More was eventually allowed to regenerate naturally and, apart from a brief spell as both a sheep and deer forest, remained almost undisturbed until this century.

In 1923 the forest was acquired by the Forestry Commission and, when it was quickly realised that timber could only be grown profitably

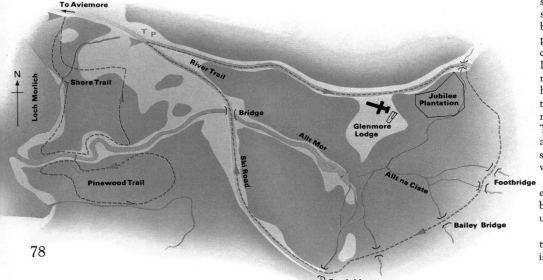

is an important winter food source for deer during the particularly long and harsh Highland winters.

Herds of red deer are not common in Glen More, but visitors are likely to come across a group of roe deer amongst the pine or birch woods. The rutting season for red deer begins in October and it is often possible to hear the boastful stags roaring in the forest clearings on a clear, autumn evening.

The roe is a shy creature and lives in small, family units. The bucks establish distinct territories within the woods and, to the great consternation of the foresters, identify their domain by fraying and stripping the young trees of their bark. The deer population can at times become too great or damage to plantations excessive and it then becomes necessary to cull the herds.

Photographers wishing to capture these magnificent beasts on film can arrange to use a forest hide for a minimal fee.

On a miniature scale, the insect population of the forest is huge and yet often goes unnoticed. The ant is a highly energetic and important woodland worker and can be seen during the summer months climbing the seemingly gigantic pine trunks and carrying a cargo of litter, resin and other insects. It is thought that the fastidiousness of the ants helps to prevent disease within the forest and visitors are asked to avoid damaging the numerous anthills. These can often be up to two feet high and may be camouflaged with leaf mould.

The mischievous red squirrel is often very tame and has learnt that visitors usually mean food – even if retrieving it means upturning a wastepaper basket or two! Their staple diet is pine seeds and often if a chewed pine cone should fall from the tree above then its a fair assumption that a cheeky squirrel, having finished his lunch, is taking a pot shot at you!

Foxes, badgers and wildcats all live in the forest but are difficult to observe; one is more likely to stumble over a badger sett, smell a fox trail or hear a wildcat cry than actually come

on the lower slopes, so rendering three-quarters of the estate unplantable, the area was created a Forest Park in 1948. Replanting took place immediately with Sitka and Norway spruce, Douglas fir, Scots and Lodgepole pine and larch. Early planting relied on manual labour and it was not until after the war that machines and fertilisers were employed in any great quantities. This factor has since had a considerable effect on the character of the woods: the pre-war areas, south of Loch Morlich, are irregular in growth and planting pattern, contrasting vividly with the uniform pattern and vigorous growth of the modern, man-made, northern woods.

Scattered throughout the 4000 acres are various stands of Caledonian Pine as monuments to the original forest cover. The pines vary in age from two to four hundred years old and can have either tall, straight trunks with luxurious leaf canopies or be much smaller, gnarled and twisted specimens. This difference is not a genetic factor but the results of varying soil types and weather conditions.

Pines are, in general, hardy species, especially when self-sown. However, the Sitka spruce, despite the fact that it was imported from the chilly climes of North America, is susceptible to frosts. There is one distinct frost pocket on the Pinewood Trail in a forest section near the Allt Mhor, where the cold air from the surrounding hills drains and here spruce are struggling to survive the adversities.

Fire can also take its toll on the forest.

Again, on the Pinewood Trail, stands a grove of pines blackened by a fire during the last war. The young saplings and thin-barked trees were all destroyed and only those older, thicker-barked trees have survived to mark the event.

Near to the shores of Loch Morlich another native British conifer has taken root. The juniper flourishes at Glen More and, apart from its brewing and culinary connections,

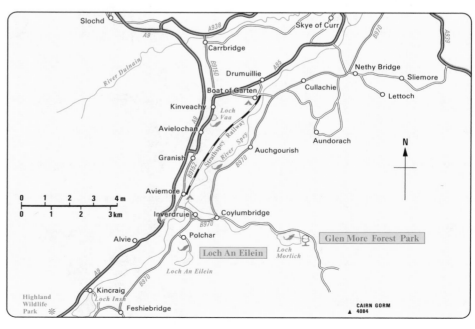

Angling
Loch Morlich: trout
fishing 5m SE of
Aviemore
Daily tickets: The
Warden, Glenmore
Forest Park
Osprey Fishing
School: Aviemore
centre offering boat
fishing on loch, with
facilities for disabled
anglers
Tel: (0479) 810767
River Spey: fine
salmon fishing
Daily tickets:
Kelman's Stores,
Boat of Garten
Tel: (0479) 983) 205
or G Mortimer, 61
High Street,
Grantown-on-Spey
Tel: (0479) 2684
Loch Vaa: fly fishing
for reasonable trout
3m SW of Boat of
Garten
Daily tickets:
Kelman's Stores (see
River Spey) or
Craigard Hotel, Boat
of Garten
Tel: (047 983) 206

Camping
Aviemore: Speyside
Caravan Park ▶▶▶
Tel: (0479) 810236
Level 104-pitch site
(no tents)
Open Apr then
Jun–Aug, no
bookings
Boat of Garten: Boat
of Garten Camping &
Caravanning
Park ▶▶▶
level 50-pitch site
Open all year (ex
Nov), no bookings

Golfing
Boat of Garten:
Tel: (047 983) 282
Parkland course with
good views, 18 holes,
5637yds, par 70,

SSS68

Riding
Nethy Bridge: Nethy
Bridge Pony Trekking
& Riding Centre (5m
SW of Grantown-on-
Spey)
Tel: (047 982) 693

Ski-ing
Aviemore:
Strathspey Hotel: ski
instruction &
equipment hire
Tel: (0479) 810681

General
Aviemore: Aviemore
Centre: vast indoor
leisure complex
including swimming
pool, ice rink, cinema
& theatre
Tel: (0479) 810264
Boat of Garten:
Strathspey Railway:
5m journey by steam
train
Open mid-May–Sep
Sat & Sun, plus Tue,
Wed & Thu Jul–Aug
Braemar: Braemar
Castle: largely rebuilt
17th-century fortress
with Son et Lumière
held late Aug–early
Sep
Open May–early Oct
daily 10–6
Tel: (033 83) 219
Kincraig: Highland
Wild Life Park: many
animals including
bears, bison, reindeer
& wolves
Open Mar–Oct daily
10–6
Tel: (054 04) 270
Tomintoul:
Tomintoul Museum:
rebuilt farm kitchen
with cobbling &
saddlery exhibits,
11m SE of Grantown-
on-Spey
Open Jun–Sep daily
Tel: (080 74) 285

The pure waters of the Spey are an important ingredient in producing Scottish malt whiskies and several distilleries in the valley open their doors to visitors. As anglers will know, the Spey's claim to fame is not in whisky alone for there are trout, sea trout and salmon to be caught in the clear waters. Further afield there are trout at Loch Vaa and Avielochan and salmon in the Feshie and Dulnain rivers. For novice anglers, there is a fishing school at the Aviemore Centre.

Aviemore, the now famous 'alpine' village is just a few minutes drive from the forest. Within the modern complex are housed an exhausting range of leisure facilities, entertainments, shops and restaurants – guaranteed to appeal to all age groups. The Centre is open for business all year round and in winter is transformed as the heart of British skiing. There are fourteen pistes, all requiring varying degrees of skill and six schools to give tuition. Chair lifts and ski-tows are in operation all day to transfer skiers to the higher slopes.

A lazier way of enjoying the valley is to hitch a ride on the Strathspey Steam Railway as it chugs backwards and forwards between Aviemore and Boat of Garten. An alternative is to view the valley on horseback; there are pony trekking centres at Carrbridge, Nethy Bridge, Laggan and Aviemore.

Keen golfers will have to resort to a car drive to follow their sport in this part of the Highlands. There are woodland and moor courses at Grantown-on-Spey, Boat of Garten, Nethy Bridge, Kingussie and Newtonmore.

Whilst in the Glen More region, visitors should certainly try to visit Loch an Eilein, some six miles south east of the forest. Here a 15th-century, ruined castle stands romantically on the tiny islet, surrounded by gently lapping waters and lush woodlands.

The lands surrounding the loch are part of the Rothiemurchus estate and the Cairngorms National Nature Reserve, however, the Nature Conservancy Council have recently established a nature trail which allows visitors to walk the entire perimeter of the loch.

The trail starts from the northern point of the water and meanders through natural Scots pine woodland rich in wildlife, small mammals and birds while the loch itself supports an abundance of brown trout, pike, eels and otters. Butterflies are colourful visitors to the loch-side meadows and dragonflies – flashing by in a haze of azure blue – are a common summertime sight.

The trail is some three miles long and, as the paths are not arduous, should take the average walker no more than two hours to complete. The Loch an Eilein area is continuously under strict surveillance as a Nature Reserve and visitors are particularly requested not to disturb the beauty and tranquillity of the area.

The loch is also under observation and is therefore out of bounds to bodies and boats alike! A loch-side cottage has been converted as an information centre and the Reserve wardens will advise on Cairngorm wildlife.

across the real thing. Persistent observers should make an early start to catch a glimpse of a fox returning to his hole after a night's hunting or sit at dusk, downwind from a badger's sett, to see the whiskered, black and white face emerge.

Visitors wishing to camp within the forest can use the Commission's own site of twenty acres backing on to the shores of Loch Morlich with 221 level, grassy pitches to choose from. There are three modern toilet blocks, a well-stocked shop, restaurant and laundry room. Alternatively there are additional sites at Boat of Garten and Aviemore.

Loch Morlich is itself a major attraction for visitors. The sandy shores are ideal for picnics or sunbathing and the waters for canoeing or sailing. The Loch also attracts a variety of water birds throughout the year; mallard, teal, widgeon, duck, swan and geese can be seen.

If you have a head for heights, view the forest from above by taking the ski lift from near the Glen More campsite to within 500 feet of the summit of Cairngorm. On a clear day the views are breathtaking; to the north is Ben Wyvis, to the south Ben Nevis and below sparkles the Spey Valley.

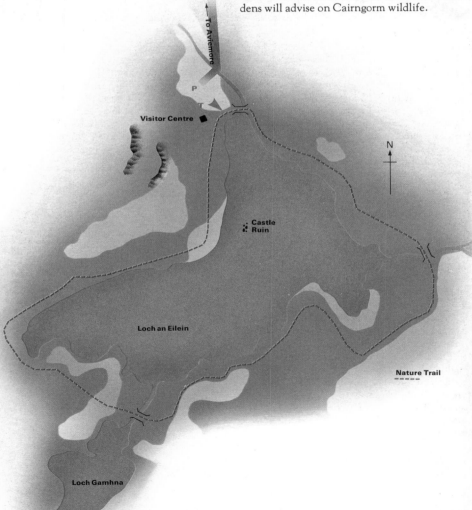